Breaking (into) the Circle

Group Work for Change in the English Classroom

Hephzibah Roskelly

Foreword by James Strickland

Boynton/Cook
HEINEMANN
Portsmouth, NH

Boynton/Cook Publishers, Inc.
A subsidiary of Reed Elsevier Inc.
361 Hanover Street
Portsmouth, NH 03801–3912
www.boyntoncook.com

Offices and agents throughout the world

The author and publisher wish to thank those who have generously given permission to reprint borrowed material:

"For Better or Worse" cartoons are reprinted by permission of Lynn Johnston Productions, Inc. Copyright © Lynn Johnston Productions, Inc.

Photograph "Child Raising His Hand on the First Day of School" is reprinted from *News & Record*, Greensboro, NC. Used by permission of the News & Record Library.

Library of Congress Cataloging-in-Publication Data
Roskelly, Hephzibah.
    Breaking (into) the circle : group work for change in the English classroom / Hephzibah Roskelly.
        p.   cm.
    Includes bibliographical references and index.
    ISBN 0-86709-543-1 (pbk. : acid-free paper)
    1. English philology—Study and teaching (Higher).   2. Group work in education.   I. Title.

    PE66 .R58 2002
    428'.0071'1—dc21   2002011731

Editor: Lisa Luedeke
Production service: TechBooks
Production coordinator: Lynne Reed
Cover design: Joni Doherty
Typesetter: TechBooks
Manufacturing: Steve Bernier

Printed in the United States of America on acid-free paper
06   05   04   03   02   DA   1   2   3   4   5

The search for the truth is in one way hard and another easy. For it is evident that no one of us can ever master it fully nor miss it wholly. Each one of us adds a little to our knowledge of nature, and from all the facts assembled arises a certain grandeur.

Aristotle

Contents

Foreword

Most teachers have heard accounts of or experienced firsthand the situation in which the school administrator becomes confused when he or she finds the teacher to be observed involved with students in small-group work. "I'll come back later, when you're teaching," the evaluator says. I heard one such account from a teacher in the 1980s, and my wife, Kathleen, heard another from a different teacher in the 1990s. In *Breaking (into) the Circle: Group Work for Change in the English Classroom*, Hephzibah Roskelly recounts her firsthand experience with such an evaluator. The message is clear: Group work is perceived as different from real teaching. Even those of us who value group work know that it is often misunderstood, not only by administrators, but also by teachers and students.

The misunderstandings begin with the "lecture in the round." Some teachers have their students move the desks into a circle in an attempt to replicate the success they see colleagues having with groups. Then, taking a chair alongside the students in the circle, these teachers proceed to monopolize the conversation. Frequently the only students who are active are those who also would have been had the desks remained in rows. Another misunderstanding is the use of small groups for what one person in our department used to refer to as *seatwork*, busywork given at the end of a class period to fill the remaining time. Often the worksheets the students are given to complete during this time could be filled in more quickly alone. If there is any talk in these groups, it is only to find the person who can supply the answers for the others. Students also misunderstand what they are to do in groups and, lacking any other strategy, mimic teacher responses, such as "Be more specific," when responding to one another's writings. An old classroom management joke is "How do you get a class to be quiet?" Answer: "Put them in groups."

Yet misunderstandings alone can't account for the hostility some teachers and students have for group work. "I tried that years ago; group work is great in theory but stinks in practice," the teachers say. "I'm the one who always gets stuck doing the work, while the rest of the bozos get the same credit I do," the students say. "And even if they do come up with something, it's usually so lame that I have to fix it anyway," our niece Kelly adds. At the heart of the student complaints is the sense of unfairness about grades, which undermine group accomplishment at every turn. "Group work ends up being more or less useless if the real or final purpose for group work is always individual achievement," Hephzibah, "Hepsie" to her friends, says in this text. The practice of awarding students a score for every category or subject at the completion of each marking period is so central to our education system that there is no way to operate outside it. It would be like having baseball without the standings, the batting averages, and the ERAs (earned run averages). You could do it, of course; but it wouldn't count. And we rarely do things that don't count. Moreover, when you get down to it, group work flies in the face of the American myth of the rugged individual. This is somewhat ironic considering that the real work of our American government is done by groups, Congress and the Supreme Court, while the attention and credit is given to the solitary leader, the President.

The problems with groups also include problems inherent to the personalities of those in the groups. Some students dominate the thought, the talk, and the work of groups. Other students volunteer or are resigned to do the bulk of the work. Still others are slackers who know how to work the system. Likewise, some teachers want to control what the groups talk about, fear chaos and anarchy, and end up squashing productive talk if it appears to be off task.

In *Breaking (into) the Circle: Group Work for Change in the English Classroom*, Hepsie reviews all these problems and misunderstandings, with sharper clarity and in greater detail than is possible in this Foreword, but then she challenges teachers to "move beyond the failures so often associated with groups and toward the transformative power the group offers to the classroom." The transformative power of group work that she speaks of promotes an attitude of caring, the development of inner speech and social speech, the use of creative play, and the formation of what Paulo Freire has called *culture circles*. Hepsie believes group work "establishes and enables making learning happen," to borrow Jeff Golub's phrase.

Unlike the three robins who just hatched outside our bedroom window, we aren't born preprogrammed for this life; we must learn from others. We spend an inordinate amount of time in school, learning and unlearning things. It's okay to forget some things. To our detriment, though, we forget other things such as the importance of learning to "play well with others." And, as with most important lessons in life, the others from whom we learn are not always those designated as such—parents and teachers—but our friends and mentors, people we trust and respect and who respect us. We "learn it on the playground," as we used to say. To help us understand what it takes to make groups work, Hepsie explains how we learn and how we interact with other people. So this is a book about epistemology and psychology as much as it is about teaching English.

Teachers who long in their hearts for productive group work will be tempted to jump right to Chapter 5, in which Hepsie reveals her blueprint for success with working in groups. However, they would be wise to resist this temptation and follow Hepsie's well-reasoned discussion of why group work is important, how learning takes place, what pitfalls can occur in group work, and how race and gender are related to the difficulties and benefits of group work.

Hepsie quotes philosopher C. S. Peirce, who has said we are not whole as long as we are single. However, I like to think of the old folk song "Will the Circle be Unbroken," which maintains that in the circle we find completion and ultimately the answers to life's questions, by and by.

James Strickland

Acknowledgments

An acknowledgments page seems especially important in a book about group work. The dozens of groups I've worked with over the years—teachers' groups, community groups, and especially the many student groups in many classrooms—have challenged and transformed my thinking about how groups can work. I'm indebted to all of them.

I have changed all names and all conversations in this book to preserve anonymity, and all student writing is anonymous as well. I thank all these students for giving permission for me to use their words in this book. Thanks to all my classes at the University of North Carolina, Greensboro—Freshman Composition, Teaching of Writing, American Literature, and graduate seminars—for providing me with such a varied and rich group experience. I wish I could list all the students' names. Thanks to the graduate students (now assistant professors at universities themselves) who generously allowed me to be part of their students' group work—especially Janet Bean, Rob Milde, Sean Butler, and Judith Szerdahelyi. Thanks to the teachers at the University of New Hampshire's Summer Writing Program who helped me think productively about the culture circle and its uses for groups and to the artists who created approximations of the culture circle drawings, Kate Roskelly and Ann May. Thanks to the teachers who sent me the questions that inform the last chapter of the book: Jane Stephens, Lynne Murray, Elizabeth Chiseri-Strater, Kate Ronald, and Warren Rochelle. And a special thank you to my husband, Michael, whose clever drawing of the Crows makes their personalities come alive on the page.

Writing about groups makes me realize how much my thinking has benefited from those who surround me: my family, colleagues, students, and friends. I have been lucky to have been a part of so many wonderful circles.

Introduction

I think the hard work of a nonracist sensibility is the boundary crossing, from safe circle into wilderness: the testing of boundary, the consecration of sacrilege. It is the willingness to spoil a good party and break the encompassing circle, to travel from the safe to the unsafe. The transgression is dizzyingly intense, a reminder of what it is to be alive.

Patricia Williams (1991, p. 129)

What is the "safe circle" in the classroom, the circle that Patricia Williams said we have to be willing to break if we're to create a "nonracist sensibility"? For Williams, a law professor at New York University, the safe circle was a space where all her students knew what was expected of them and where they knew what to expect from their teacher. Her achievement-driven law students wanted badly to get information they could use—for grades and for the battery of tests they would face on their way to law degrees and prestigious jobs. Her class was indeed a safe circle, until she decided to break it by bringing into the classroom the real lives of those affected by laws, by insisting that personal story become part of evidence, and by offering challenges to the myths of justice and equality that her students assumed.

In part, teachers have always wanted to make their classrooms safe circles, locations where we tell ourselves that everybody has an equal chance and where individual personalities or backgrounds don't make any difference to the work of study and performance. But we know even as we say it that it's untrue. Persons intrude on this space, real persons with problems and personalities and skills and fears. It's impossible not to look at the persons in a class even as we deny looking. "I don't see color anymore," one student told me. "I don't think I ever did." "I don't care how many women there are on my syllabus," one teacher said, "as long as they're good writers, that's the important thing." "I see my students the same." We desire sameness because we desire equality.

But we haven't yet figured out how to see difference and equality together. Our students have expectations for their roles and for ours, just as we have expectations of them. Insofar as everybody understands these expectations, it's a safe circle.

To the extent that students' lives don't match those of one another or that of the teacher, or the myth of the student or the classroom activity, the classroom can't be safe. Too many experiences and opinions and values get shut down or closed out. We lose these students, even if we're unaware of it. Only when we acknowledge difference and use it can the classroom become what it needs to be, a place of trust where we can together cross from the safe circles of unquestioned assumptions into the wilderness of new ideas and divergent experience and opinion.

Teachers and students have to be ready to break the circle of sameness that prevents voices from being heard and ideas being questioned, to spoil the "good party" where lines are clearly drawn between an A and a B, between what counts as knowledge and what doesn't. Only then can difference be a positive, energizing factor in the classroom, only then can we create the kind of trust that can lead to engaged learning, or real literacy. The strategy that can do this most effectively and profoundly, I believe, is use of the small group. As its own circle, the small group can break up the space that keeps students and teachers and ideas in their preordained places. In conversation with one another, students learn to cross the boundaries that have kept them passive learners, sleepy thinkers, and fearful writers. As Williams described this new space, it *is* a wilderness: where nothing is certain, where the answers aren't really waiting, and where chaos and trouble might ensue. The wilderness is scary for both students and teachers, for there's always the possibility of wandering far too long with no clear destination in sight. It's open rather than closed, this new circle, and this means anything can happen.

But the rewards are great for the "transgression." Williams called the process "dizzyingly intense." Considering the groups I've worked with, I'd say that's a fair statement. When students recognize that their work together can change the course of the discussion, or of the class, or of their own thinking, it's a rush. They become invested in their own learning, aware and conscious that they are making meaning. And teachers become invested in helping the change happen, in facilitating a conversation that can create such transformation. The teachers and students you'll hear from in this book describe this process.

Does this investment in the group sound too grand or too hopeful? Can the small group really make all that much of a difference in the way we see ourselves in the classroom, or in the way we think outside it? In this book, I try to suggest how it might make such a difference by looking at the work of many small groups, most of which I've taught. You'll see represented not only freshmen groups, students at the beginning of their college careers, but also graduate groups, students at the end of theirs. Many teachers and many soon-to-be teachers were in the groups I wrote about. There are students of writing and of literature, students who were taking courses to fill requirements, and students who were there because they love the subject. I think the work of each of these small groups has made a difference to the thinking and writing of the individuals who have composed them.

Group work is a familiar strategy, almost too familiar since many teachers and students have bad memories of unfortunate group experiences in their pasts. But as a philosophy, group work has been insufficiently examined. In fact, I argue that the reason for so many failed groups is that there has been so little discussion of the philosophical dimension—the rationale for groups and their possibilities. There has been little discussion of method as well. And although this is not a how-to book, I want to pay attention to the very real considerations that can ensure a group's failure and those that can nurture the possibilities for its success.

We break the circle that holds us in place and we break into new circles where we find new places. This is the work of the small group. And the work of education.

Chapter One

Group Work Matters

The Stage Is Set

The English 101 classroom I walked into in fall 1996 was what some educators might call typical: twenty-three students, most just out of high school. Looking around the room, I counted ten males and thirteen females, nine of whom were African Americans. The African American students sat near one another, with five at one table, two at another, and the other two (who had come a little late) at tables where they could find a chair.

The room was too large and too long, and students seemed more separated by the tables they sat around than connected by them. Chairs stood on top of unused tables in the back of the room, as if our class were a storeroom or due to be cleaned at any moment. The students were quiet, obviously ready for me to tell them our agenda for the semester. Many of them were also nervous, although this characteristic was less immediately obvious than others. Yet their nervousness manifested itself in shy glances at the others at their table and in their still faces with occasional small giggles. They physically straightened themselves when I walked into the room, which signaled to me and to one another that the work was about to begin. I was about to tell them what the work was to be.

I walked among the tables first, asking questions about the books they had on the table or about their hometown, small talk to get the classroom conversation going. They smiled and answered politely, one or two offering a comment or a question. I moved back to the front of the room and faced them. "How long have you been college students?" I asked them. "Three hours," one said, and the others laughed. I told them about my daughter, who was beginning college sixty miles down the

1

road. I asked them how it felt so far. All this talk seemed easy, but I knew it was a little unnerving too. Some of them glanced down at their notebooks, or at one another, no doubt wondering when they'd hear the bad news about how many papers, how many books, how many absences. They were waiting, their expressions told me clearly, for me to give the commands, set up the regulations, tell them their tasks—which they would greet, their expressions also told me, with some degree of dismay.

I turned to the blackboard, too far away from most of the students, and began to write with chalk the consistency of wax. The words were so light they were nearly indecipherable. I laughed and told the students they'd have to learn to be good translators, as I wrote my phone number and the names of the textbooks and began at last to describe the course and the syllabus they now held in their hands.

"It's a writing course," I told them. "Guess what we'll do next time in class?" They all got it quickly. Write. And they all smiled. I nodded agreement. "And guess what we'll do after that?" No answer for a minute. Then, "Look at our grades?" And then, "Revise what we've written?" "Make us read what we wrote out loud?"

"No," I said. "We get into our groups." (See Figure 1–1.)

* * *

I've discovered over the years that my students are more or less united in their attitudes toward groups, and this group of first-year writers was no different. Students like the idea of forming little circles in the big unit of the classroom; they like the idea that they might get to talk to somebody besides the teacher. But they are unlikely to believe that the work they might do in a group will matter very much to them or be very valuable in the scheme of the class. They've been conditioned to see group work as a technique for getting them to know one another ("Are we going to tell three things about ourselves and then get introduced?" one student said to me as I broke them into groups for the second day of our class), for allowing the teacher to stop talking, or for simply breaking up the day. But they've not seen groups related explicitly to learning or to improving the quality of the learning they'll do in the classroom. They certainly don't see groups as a way to change or transform their writing or reading or their attitudes about themselves and one another. My students in freshman composition gather into their groups the first time with what I perceive as resignation; they clearly regard this part of the class as a typical teacher's tactic to get them to do what she's already decided they must do. They'll break into their groups, and willingly, since they at least get to move a little and abandon their rapt staring at the front of the room. But they don't relish it particularly, because they don't believe that it matters particularly.

Figure 1–1 English 101, day 2: Division of class into groups

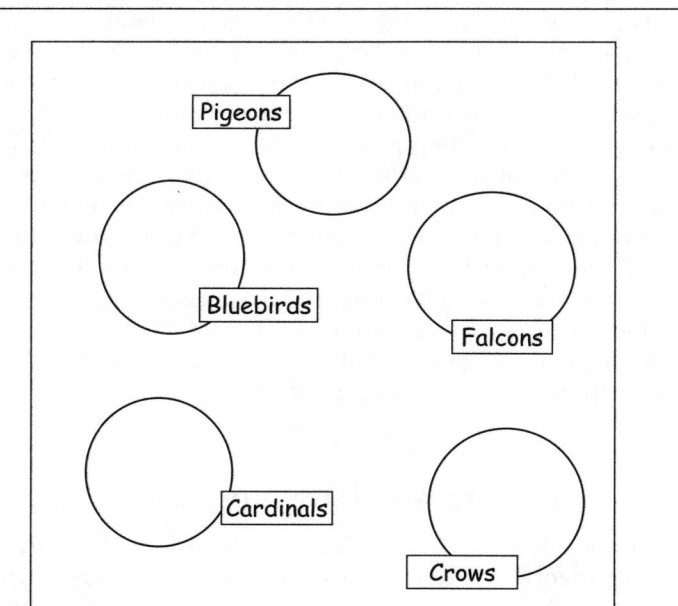

This feeling, common among the students I've taught over the past two decades, holds despite twenty-five years and more of encouragement from teachers and theorists to make group work a part of the work of the classroom at all levels and in all subjects. Social construction theories—ranging from the work of Jean Piaget and Lev Vygotsky to the more recent studies by Jill McLean Taylor, Carol Gilligan, and Amy Sullivan; Karen Burke LeFevre; and Kenneth Bruffee—demonstrate, with their careful experimentation and observation of learners at work, the ways in which the individual's ability to solve problems, acquire new information, and increase knowledge is enhanced in an informal social setting. Teachers, picking up on the researchers' understandings, have written movingly about how working together transforms the students' individual accomplishments. Paulo Freire, Geneva Smitherman, Nancie Atwell, Nel Noddings, and many other teachers of students at all levels make group endeavor central to their literacy programs.

Yet, in my institution, group work is used sparingly. Except in the first-year composition class, whose program I direct, group work is discussed positively but enacted rarely, save for the specialized instance of the creative writing workshop. Teachers at university levels cite the necessity for coverage, the exigencies of large classes at basic levels of instruction, and the problems with evaluating performance, among other reasons, for their veering away from using group work in their classrooms. Similarly, in the high schools where I observe student teachers, group work is seldom attempted successfully, and student teachers are often actively discouraged from trying to put groups to work for them in their unit or lesson plans. Their cooperating teachers tell me that group work often makes classroom management more difficult, that they themselves have found that the effort involved in keeping groups on task exceeds the benefits of having groups work together, especially when there is so much material to be covered. "I used to use groups a lot with the good classes especially," one teacher told me. "I've given it up even with them. It's just not worth it."

How to Make Groups Worth It

Why a strategy for teaching and learning that is resoundingly endorsed by literacy theories is so unsuccessful in practice designed to support literacy is, at first glance, puzzling. Some people might suggest that theories are always out of touch with practice. The "what looks good on paper..." argument touches a chord in all teachers who've seen theories and strategies in educational mandates come and go with bewildering speed and disheartening consistency. But that gap is simply not sufficient to explain teachers' inability to make group work an organic part of the classroom work, especially since teachers themselves recognize the potential benefits of group work for their students and for their own programs of instruction. One goal of this book is to uncover the attitudes and issues that prevent groups from becoming an effective tool for teachers and for their students. The predominant goal of this book, however, is to locate new, more helpful strategies for teachers to use as they design courses and lessons that make real use of groups.

One premise of this book is that theory and practice must—and do—interact in every lesson plan and classroom activity teachers design and carry out. Sometimes theory matches practice so well that teachers may believe there's no theory involved, such as when a teacher notices that the farther back the students sit, the less attention they pay to him or her (distance signals lack of involvement for many students; this theoretical belief guides teachers either to force students to sit close or to place potential troublemakers close to the front of the room). Other times there's such a mismatch between belief and action that the practice feels uncomfortable or wrong. Mandates from school systems about instruction, including testing, fall under this category. Teachers are seldom informed about rationales for some of these system-inspired activities but are simply required to apply them and are sometimes even punished for not applying them well enough.[1]

The primary reason that group work so often fails when it's attempted is that the practice of using groups conflicts with theories about knowledge and achievement that teachers, students, and institutions hold on to, most often unconsciously. How can a student be simultaneously collaborative and competitive with others? How can a teacher be at once the authority and the novice? How can achievement be evaluated in a context in which individual achievement counts for little? These and other troubling questions lie just under the surface of teachers' worries about group work and students' lack of confidence in the worth of group work. The aim of this book is to find ways to make the theories of literacy and literary or culture study change practices, and to make these new practices not only conscious but dynamic, ready to change the theories teachers and students hold in their heads when they enter the classroom.

As Paulo Freire continually argued throughout his life as a teacher of literacy, education should come not from abstract theories but from the concrete practices of people's lives. His insistence on experience, on action, as the heart and the test of theory is what he called *praxis*. "Critical consciousness," he noted in *The Politics of Education* (1985), is brought about "not through an intellectual effort alone but through praxis—through the authentic union of action and reflection" (p. 36). Freire's belief in practice is tied to a consequent belief in theory: practice is the final test and the goal for theory, but theory guides and challenges practice. And the two must combine in conscious, systematic ways for *conscientitizao*, "critical consciousness," to occur. It is finally critical consciousness, the ability to see oneself acting in a world that is dynamic rather than static, that makes a person literate.

Freire's argument about the necessary link between theory and practice, and the necessary accommodation of theories to practices, provides a method for seeing how group work's goals can be translated into actual changed practice in the classroom. Groups by necessity accommodate the various experiences group members bring to the group.

---

1. The ABC program in North Carolina is one such mandate, designed to improve student scores by pushing teacher accountability. The program rewards teachers with monetary bonuses for their students' high test scores on standardized statewide tests and punishes teachers and schools for low scores with threats of intervention from state agencies who put schools on warning lists and outline required procedures for improvement. For details on NC's reform movement in education, see, for example, "ABC Is Latest Solution," Greensboro *News & Record*, Greensboro, NC, Aug. 24, 1997; pp. F. 3.

"Educators Give ABC a Good Grade." News & *Observer*, Raleigh, NC; June 13, 1996, p. A. 3.

"Rewards for Reform, *News & Observer*, Raleigh, NC; April 9, 1996, p. A. 8.

Groups must, as a result, listen, pay attention to differences; they must change course or redesign plans depending on group members' perspectives and the sharing of these perspectives. And the classroom itself must alter to reflect the change in conversation that happens when groups provide reports of their work together to the larger group. As each group hears from the others, they learn even more about the topics at hand and about how knowledge is being made in the other small circles around them. Theories of instruction, of how knowledge occurs and is made, of how students behave and teachers talk, become infused with new ideas that emerge from the new experience that results from much talk and new activity.

The Need for Groups

The need for changed practice in classrooms is great: students at all levels and from all backgrounds suffer in an educational system that denies them agency, that refuses to accommodate itself to their unique experiences, ideas, hopes, and needs. This appears to be especially true of the students in U.S. society who are placed on the margins of academic culture—poverty-stricken students, students from minority ethnic groups, students afflicted by a racist and persistently sexist society. A recent national educational report documents this problem. The College Board's National Task Force on Minority High Achievement, a group composed of leading educators from colleges and high schools across the United States, compiled the results of an array of research that showed a continuing performance gap that exists between students of color—African American, Hispanic, and American Indian students—and their white and Asian counterparts. The gap persists throughout students' schooling, the study showed, from kindergarten to graduate school. Even worse, the difference in achievement cannot be accounted for by socioeconomic factors alone. Gaston Caperton, the president of the College Board who initiated the Task Force, noted, "It is particularly troubling because we are not just talking about disadvantaged youngsters. Even minority students from relatively wealthy families with well-educated parents do not typically perform as well as white and Asian students from similar backgrounds" ("Report Examines Minority Underachievement," 1999).

Some of the Task Force's findings are these: Although minorities make up about thirty percent of the under- eighteen population, only ten percent of fourth-, eighth-, and twelfth-grade students who scored at the highest levels on the National Assessment of Educational Progress tests in reading, math, and science were minorities. Minorities earn significantly lower grades than those of white and Asian students in mainstream colleges and universities, even when they score similarly on college entrance exams. Among black students, men are awarded only 36% of the college degrees. The Task Force noted that the rapid changes in racial and ethnic composition in the United States, where by the year 2030 minorities will compose over forty percent of the population under eighteen, "bring a new sense of urgency" to the work of closing this gap.

Despite decades of discussion about meeting the needs of disadvantaged students and despite hundreds of programs in colleges and schools designed to meet these needs, education has been unable to help these students achieve more. Even more distressing is that, according to the report, none of these programs has even identified the problem. Why should students of color even from relatively wealthy or stable environments achieve at such lower rates than those of others? Why should so fewer complete their education? Why should so many more of these students get worse grades? The Task Force recommendations include calls for schools to share information that improves minority achievement and for colleges and universities to collaborate more directly with high schools. But it seems that teachers and schools need to look within as well, at the way their classrooms reward and punish, at the way difference is valued and dismissed, and at the lives of the students themselves.

The system of public education is a good reflection of the systems outside it, and as such it remains both oppressively, if unconsciously, sexist and racist. The now-famous 1994 American Association of University Women (AAUW) report "Higher Education: A Chilly Climate for Women" and the 1994 exhaustively researched *Failing at Fairness: How America's Schools Cheat Girls* by David and Myra Sadker document how persistent and widespread sexism is in classrooms. Both studies confirm how women are dismissed in classrooms and how curricula ignore or downplay women's achievements. Johnathan Kozol emphatically demonstrated in *Savage Inequalities* (1991) and *Amazing Grace* (1995) how unremitting racism is as well, in his ethnographic look at inner-city schools and the conditions of public schooling where the majority of students are from racial and ethnic minorities.

For all kinds of reasons, including the roles society has assigned them, females find ways of achieving in schools, even under the circumstances the AAUW report and the Sadkers' study uncover. But it isn't much of a leap to imagine that many students of color, systematically excluded from the circle of academic respectability and achievement, begin to choose their own circles, outside the schoolyards. The real hope of group work lies in the possibility it can offer for nurturing more equitable systems within the classroom and the institution—more equal spaces for all the members who are invited to break into the academic circle—that is, all students who enter public schools.

In *The Challenge to Care in Schools* (1992), Nel Noddings argued that students' increasing lack of knowledge of the "basics"—in geography, history, English, and math—derives from their lack of *caring* about these subjects and the basic facts about them. Schools, she noted, are teaching very much the same subjects as they were fifty years ago. Walk into any high school English classroom, and you'll hear words you remember from your high school days: *topic sentence, denouement, subject-verb agreement, secondary source.* But students aren't attending to them. As one of my colleagues at the university where I teach once said to me despairingly, "I'm teaching them, Hepsie, but they're just not learning." As Noddings made clear, many students cannot find a reason to bother with standard subject matter. But, she said, "With sufficient attention to their own felt needs and interests, most students would pick up items of general culture just as many children do in family life" (p. 36). The performance gap reported by the College Board's Task Force might close or shorten with attention to some of these "felt needs."

How do we give such attention? How do teachers and students connect? And, in this day of increasing difference in age, outlook, and background in both high school and college classrooms, how might such connection happen among students themselves? Noddings said, "Kids learn in communion. They listen to people who matter to them and to whom they matter. The patterns of ignorance we deplore today are signs that kids and adults are not talking to each other about everyday life and the cultural forms once widely shared" (pp. 36–37).

Group work promotes precisely this kind of communion and caring when it's initiated and sustained in an organic, integral part of classroom learning. When teachers learn how and why group work fosters the kind of literacy that makes students into active, engaged learners, they begin their own process of *conscientitizao*, and they learn how to make their classrooms become environments where communication—and communion—can happen.

The Process of Finding Communion

The communion and communication mentioned in the previous section is not easy to come by, especially in a class like my English 101 course, which lasts fifteen weeks and which students sandwich in between work—sometimes up to forty hours of it—and four other courses. A sense of belonging is difficult to nurture in a classroom so anonymous and unwelcoming and among students whose lives suddenly seem so separate from those of one another: different majors, different living arrangements, different reasons for being in college. But I look back at the work of the group of 101 students that fall in 1996, and I find reason to believe that the painstaking effort needed to engender and maintain good working groups is worth it, that change can and does occur. Not neatly. Not universally. But clearly.

I'm looking at the manila folders of my student groups for my 101 class. At the beginning of the semester, I give each group a folder that will house their collaborative work. It's a visible reminder to the groups and to me that the work we accomplish in small circles is real work, that it can be examined and used. I collect these folders at the end of each class period and read and comment on any work the group has accomplished. At the end of the semester when students are compiling portfolios, I ask them to write a reflection of their work in the group, and they use the group folder to help them comment.

The first folder I'm reviewing is from the Falcons. I begin the semester by giving each group a name. I always give the groups bird names, a reprise of the students' earliest experiences with group names in kindergarten or first grade. I ask them about the names for their first reading groups in school. I find that some groups are still titled with bird names, as mine was when I was in first grade. "Bluebirds were best," I tell them. One student calls out, "In our class it was the Tigers who were." And another says, "We got to name ourselves. We were the Millennium Falcons. But we knew we weren't the good group anyway." We talk a lot about names as we begin the semester's work. The first writing assignment—in fact, an in-class writing that they will all share in their groups—asks them to comment on the beginning of Sandra Cisneros' "The House on Mango Street," the section that's titled "My Name is Esperanza." I use this idea of the importance of names and naming as we begin our study of cultural myths and metaphors that forms the basis of most of our reading during the semester.

The Falcon's folder is labeled in large letters FALCON PRIDE. There's a drawing of a falcon, I think, below the name, and then the names of each of the five students who made up the group—Camille, Rebecca, Tawanna, Stephanie. They had crossed out Joe's name because he left the class, and school, after the first few weeks of the semester. The Falcons were a lively group, three African American young women and one white woman, all of whom loved to laugh and talk. And eat. I had to ask them to stop bringing Chinese food to class unless they intended to share it with all the other groups. They wrote with varying degrees of assurance and skill, and they all gathered confidence from one another. "Talking about our myths was a way for us to 'relive' what happened to us," they wrote in a reflection in their folder. "We figured out how to be more vivid on paper, the way we talk!" The three other groups wrote similar comments in their folders. The Cardinals, the Bluebirds (I see in the corner that the one male in the group wrote "Micah's Bluebirds"), and the Pigeons, who gave themselves that bird name, liked their group work, judging from their folders' comments. I know that there were successes and failures among them as they worked, that some found new voices, that a few didn't, that they worked hard or let work slide, but that they finished the class knowing one another and knowing something about one another's point of view in writing. That feels significant.

I'd like to analyze in a little more detail the workings of these groups, looking at some of their writing, and talking about what happened to them individually and collectively as the semester progressed. Using one small-group example might help underscore the theoretical suppositions about group work and the arguments that underlie the call for groups in the classroom.

Listening to the Crows

The fifth group in the 101 class called themselves the Crows. I think I had given them the name Canaries or something innocuous, but as they met for the first time, they decided they needed a name that reflected something more about them. Crows, they all agreed, and affirmed when the class laughed as they announced themselves, were birds with an attitude, birds who asserted themselves. Their naming themselves in the first meeting indicated how accurate their new title was. (The Pigeons changed their bird designation a few meetings later.) The members of this group wanted to name themselves in the classroom as somehow different, maybe, like the crows they liked, a little more hip or dangerous than the rest. Adrian was living at home and commuting to school forty-five minutes each day. Smiling and seemingly shy, she mentioned how much she had liked her high school English class and how well she had performed in the class. "I love English," she said to her group. "It was my best subject." "Not me," said Marcia, and grimaced. Marcia was a music major whose alto resonated in the room. African American and from a small town at the other end of the state, Marcia was the only student in the class who was not a freshman. She had waited till now to take freshman composition because "I hate to write." Marcia had a ready wit and energy and appeared to be the group leader during the first few class meetings. The other two students were male: Shelby was a student from out of state whose quiet demeanor was belied by the jokes he told his group every day to make them break into laughter at some point during class. Stewart was an art major, a twin, his group found out the first day, whose brother was attending college with him. Stewart drew every class period as his group worked, drew as I talked, drew when he was completing our in-class writing. His drawings were intricate, cartoon caricatures that demonstrated talent and a sense of humor. He often drew while the group talked, but his responses indicated that he was listening and thinking about the flow of the conversation.

The Crows seemed to me to be a fairly dysfunctional group for the first several weeks of the semester. Marcia seemed assertive but somehow withdrawn from the group, as though her demographics made her too different to connect with the others. She talked with her group about the readings (one of the first activities we initiated in groups), shared her writing (something she was uncomfortable with at first), and responded to the others' writing, but her comments often indicated a kind of resignation with the group's activity and the outcomes. Adrian's writing problems turned out to be much more severe than her positive memories about her English class and her work would indicate. Surface-level problems in sentence boundaries, word choice, and spelling made her drafts hard to read, and Marcia and Shelby contented themselves with telling her to use her spell checker and to "be more specific." (I have discovered that in writing workshops "be more specific" is the comment uttered most often between one student and another. Often students are unsure how or why they should be specific, but they know it's a characteristic highly valued by English teachers. They often say it hesitatingly, not to offend, "You might be more specific in some places," and not to be too specific themselves.) As the semester progressed, it was clear that Adrian was discouraged by my comments on her papers, and even more so by her midterm letter, in which I commented on her work and gave her a C for her *gradesofar.*

Shelby and Stewart seemed to be much alike at first. Both seemed to be willing enough as long as what they were asked to do didn't take too much effort or engagement, and they were good enough as writers that they could pick and choose comments from their group about their writing and understand easily what my comments might suggest about reseeing a draft. But they both appeared a little bored and slightly put off by the idea of negotiating and collaborating in a small group. The two of them sometimes physically held themselves away from the two women, backing up their chairs as far as they could move, or turning so that the other group members could see only a profile view rather than a full-face view. Shelby made lots of quiet jokes, Stewart drew, and Marcia and Adrian attempted to carry on a discussion. At least that's the way it seemed to me.

One thing most teachers are at least unconsciously aware of is the way they draw conclusions about students on the basis of brief encounters, subtle movements, offhand comments, and accents, expressions, and dress. These ethnographic clues often govern the way we respond to students in conversation and in writing, and help us make decisions about activities, assignments, and presentations—the work the class will do. Insofar as this quick inquiry helps teachers think about students, it's both good and useful. But when it's done without much conscious thought—as I did with the Crows—the inquiry becomes self-limiting.

My reactions to Shelby and Stewart were based on small bits of behavior and stance that led me to see them as potential slackers, and I carried that feeling—not expressed consciously—with me as I moved around the room and talked to the Crows, as I responded to writing from the two, and as I engaged them in conversation. And I saw Shelby and Stewart as nearly the same person, with the same attitudes and skills, because their behavior in their group suggested similarities. The point is: I helped program them to respond as they did in their group and in class by my well-meant but too-quick assessment.

Each time groups meet I ask them to write small reports of what they've done, especially if they're responding to drafts or coming up with ideas for writing. Following is a sample from the Crows, written by Shelby:

> We talked about the images which we put down on paper. We gave each other hints as to what would be best to enhance the images and details. Then we talked about the elaborate details you could add in emergency room experiences. This was started by my image of an emergency room. I feel we got a lot accomplished.

Shelby's response to the group work indicated that he was working to make sense of the day's activity and was engaged in the work of the group. And it showed that he understood how his contribution made a difference to the work of the group: "This was started by my image . . ." Shelby's recognition of the part he might play in helping the group come up with and develop ideas for writing was clear. That awareness is something I didn't see when I assessed the Crows as a group.

Stewart, too, carried strengths and interests into the group. Figure 1–2 shows an early group task, in which students were asked to identify cultural stereotypes of the Old West as they prepared to read an essay on the West and an excerpt from a Western novel. You can see Stewart's hand and humor at work on the list. At this point his engagement was on the level of his own interests, and it remained there for the semester. But he stayed with the work, writing with his group and producing his own adequate essays throughout the semester. He wrote about a plan for a paper on a myth: "Guns as freedom. In the Old West, guns were everywhere, you had to have one; today some people think the same thing. Guns may have meant you stayed alive on the frontier, but you could die today." Stewart's beginning idea of how contemporary Americans, still enthralled by the Old West's myths of freedom and power, remain enamored of guns is a provocative and useful beginning for an essay. His group commented favorably, although Shelby spoke up for guns as necessary evils in twentieth-century society, giving Stewart directions for further inquiry. Adrian— or maybe Shelby—also wrote, "You could look at that old movie we saw

Figure 1–2 Early group task: Identifying cultural stereotypes of the Old West

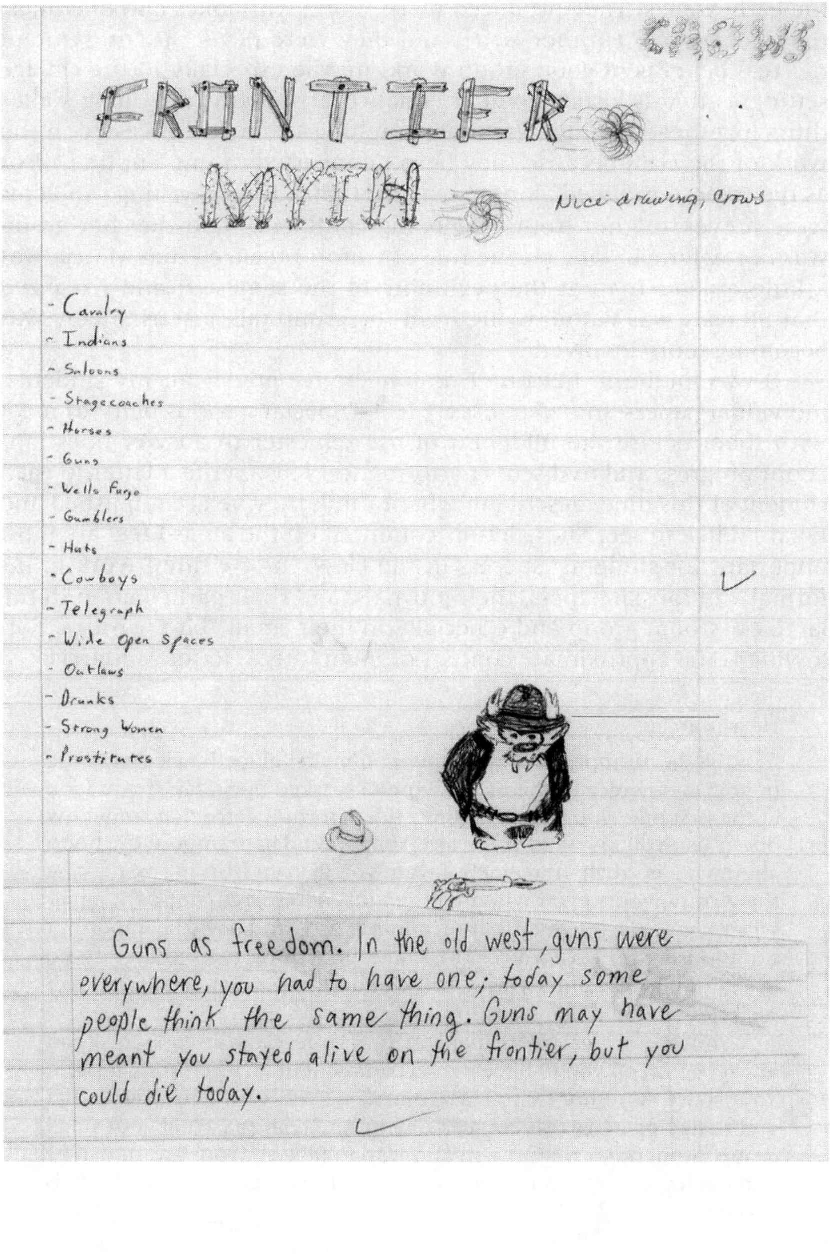

(*Stagecoach*, 1939) again, and describe the scene where they throw John Wayne the gun."

The Crows, in fact, were more functional than I had imagined in the early weeks. They produced work, along with jokes and drawings; they helped one another write; and they were never absent. (One of the real benefits of good group work, maybe especially in the college setting, is that it fosters good attendance. If students are doing something together—talking, planning, laughing—they feel invested in the work of the class because they become invested in one another.) But as the semester moved along, I realized that Adrian's writing problems were preventing her from developing confidence and that her group was not willing to take on the role of editor; I realized that Marcia was a little quieter than at the beginning of the semester; and I realized that Stewart was withdrawing from the group talk just as Shelby was becoming more involved.

It was midterm. Because I no longer give grades for my students' individual papers and responses, I feel a special responsibility to meet with them before the midpoint of the semester to answer questions about progress and to discuss performance. I also write a letter to each student at this time, describing what I think they've accomplished and what I'd like to see. These letters comment on the areas I feel are most important for students' success in the class: their written work in informal and formal papers, their journals, and their participation in the large classroom group and especially in their small "bird" groups. Following is the approximate content of my midterm letter to Marcia:

> Dear Marcia:
>
> I've been impressed with how you've developed a clearer sense of your own voice in the papers you've worked on so far. If you look at the first one, you hear a kind of stilted, formal voice that somehow doesn't let you say what you want. Your second paper, about the myth about you, is much more lively. I want you to keep working on making the writing yours even when you're writing research: our next paper will ask you to use evidence from another text, and it will be important not to lose your own voice. You could be writing more than you do in your journal: I think you're still wondering a little what I want. Let me know if you'd like ideas for journal entries.
>
> You are a great participant in our large class discussion. I can always count on you to have a good comment or an interesting insight. Your sense of humor helps make our class lively. But I've noticed that you're having more trouble speaking up and being a part of your small group. Sometimes it's just you and Adrian talking. Your group will be making its presentation soon, so you want to make sure everybody is involved.

We'll talk more about these things when I see you next week. Keep working. You're doing well, and I know you'll continue to improve during this last half of the semester.

Hepsie

gradesofar: C+

This is a fair representation of the letter I sent to Marcia (I no longer have the original, only my notes on students' progress) in which I commented on her work in the class so far. (Notice that I call it one word, *gradesofar:* I want students to see the grade for what it is, a progress report rather than a part of an average.) When Marcia received the letter, she came up to me after class to tell me she was upset with her grade. She and I met in conference the next week and talked about her grade as well as about her work in her group, which was her major concern about my letter.

In fact, when Marcia came for her appointment with me, she arrived with Adrian, and I asked them if they'd like to talk to me together. They did, maybe feeling that there was strength in numbers since both young women had received gradessofar that they were unhappy with (Adrian had a C at the midpoint) and they wanted to confront me about it. They had both brought their folders, with writing they had accomplished during the first few weeks of the semester. Together we looked at Marcia's folder: my comments indicate some problems with sentence structure, a tendency to slide over the details of her argument, and a hesitancy about using her own voice. She and I reworked a few sentences. Then Adrian began to talk: "I know I'm not the best writer, though I really loved my English class in high school and I did great in it. We didn't write that much though." But, both women said, they were stymied by not getting helpful feedback from their other group members and by feeling that they did too much of the group's work. "Shelby just nods at us and then tells jokes, and just sometimes he tells me what I might change in my paper," Marcia said. And Stewart? "He listens, but he doesn't really say much." We talked a little more about their role in the group, what they each contributed, and how they might make the group time more effective for them. I encouraged them to come back and talk or get help if they wanted. They left, feeling a little comforted by my reminder that there was still plenty of time for improvement.

Shelby's appointment with me centered on his talking about his writing and what he wanted to change about it for his final portfolio. He seemed animated, interested, more engaged in the discussion of writing and reading than I had seen him either in the class at large or in the Crows' meetings. During our conversation, I realized that Shelby felt freer to talk about these interests outside the group. He and Stewart seemed more alike in the group, and I began to see that Shelby was performing for Stewart in his group, mirroring Stewart's tone and stance in his own. I talked to him gently about working hard in his group and reminded him of the presentation coming up. When he stood up, he shook hands with me.

Stewart missed our first meeting and arrived sheepishly late at the next one. He was laughing a little, but embarrassed, and he knew I would talk to him about his somewhat distracted attitude. His writing was the most sophisticated in the group, with a clear, direct voice and a sense of how to use evidence to support an emerging idea. His sense of humor was obvious even in his serious pieces, and his control over his reading was evident as well. He nodded and ducked his head when I told him what a fine writer he seemed and how much I wanted him to be part of the group and invested in his work. He told me a little about his art major and about his twin brother who was in school with him. He thought he might do better in the second half of the term.

Reviewing the Crows' Presentation

As one of the main assignments after the midpoint of the semester, each group was asked to select an essay from the anthology we used that year in freshman composition, the short version of David Bartholomae and Anthony Petrosky's *Ways of Reading*. Each group had the task of deciding on an essay that engaged them, reading it as a group, and then making a presentation to the class that touched on some of the thematic and rhetorical issues our class had been discussing the first half of the semester. Each group was asked to use as many tools as they could muster to help the class participate in a discussion and leave the class understanding the text's ideas as well as how these ideas might connect to issues they had already discussed or were working on in their own papers.

The Crows chose to read and discuss Clifford Geertz's (1983) "The Balinese Cock Fight," perhaps the most difficult essay in the collection of readings. They wrote a note to me about why they had selected this one: "We choose the 'Balinese Cock Fight' to present. We like the voice on the first page, and it will be fun to read about cockfighting, which is illegal in this country, even though some of us know where it goes on in North Carolina." I was surprised at their choice, but gratified, and I sat in on one of their planning sessions when they assigned parts and planned for questions. They seemed clear about their goals, and for the first time I saw Adrian offering ideas and volunteering to record the ideas of her fellow group members. The essay was clearly hard for them to read, and I watched them puzzling out Geertz's words and ideas. Marcia was taking control of the group during this session, and Shelby was adding details. They were making sense of the difficult text by telling stories of cockfights they had seen on television or, in Marcia's case, a cockfight on a farm outside her hometown.

The day of the presentation, they began with a good introduction that explained Bali and Clifford Geertz. Shelby and Adrian wrote on the board, and Marcia directed the class to a particular page for comment. Stewart was absent. The group didn't seem unduly upset by his being gone, nor did they comment other than to say he had drawn the picture of the fight that they had taped to the blackboard as they began. The plan for the presentation was clear. They asked students to consider the strange cultural phenomenon that Geertz's essay describes and how the strange becomes familiar when a person becomes part of the culture itself. Shelby considered cultural phenomena in the United States that someone from outside might see as strange, and soon the class was contributing examples.

Together, they did an admirable job, talking together, interrupting productively, laughing with the class. Suddenly, near the end of their

Figure 1–3   The crows on stage during Midsemester essay presentation

talk, I looked at them and noticed: They had all worn plaid. They had all worn baseball hats—even Marcia, who liked to dress up and would never, I was sure, wear a baseball hat on her own (Figure 1–3). They had bonded, and it showed in the work they produced.

Their new feeling of community was evident in the comments they made after the event. I always ask students for two documents when their group presents: an outline of their agenda for the presentation along with any handouts they offer the class, and, the next class period, a reflection on the effect of their presentation and what they themselves had contributed to the project's success.

*   *   *

The Crows wrote their outline and handed it in with their handouts at the end of their presentation. It looked like this:

> Introduction:
> Clifford Geertz, who he is and why he wrote about the Balinese—Marcia
>> The Raid—Marcia
>> Of Cocks and Men—Adrian
>> The Fight—Adrian and Shelby
>> Odds and Even Money, how the betting works—Stewart (did not present)
>> Playing with Fire—Shelby
> Conclusion
> One of our journal entries:
> The cockfight was symbolic of the Balinese culture. How did the fight symbolize the social and ethical aspects of life in Bali? We'll ask the class to talk about this and read from our journals about what we thought.

Assessing What the Crows Learned

In their final reflections, group members each mentioned how well the group worked together and how much they liked being in front of the class as a group. They talked about getting the class involved. Some of their reflections follow:

- "It went better than I thought. We were worried about time. I was in charge of making the outline, but it was a real group effort."

- "I don't think overall that anyone drug their feet or pulled the load on this project, though we were disappointed that Stewart missed it."

- "We gave each other hints as to what would be best to enhance the images and details in the story. We talked about how elaborate it all was, and we tried to think of our own examples. We helped each other."

If the Crows found their collective voice as they took the stage for their presentation, they also realized how much they depended on one another to produce it. They were disappointed in Stewart, but loyally downplayed their dismay in their written comments and in their discussions with me. Of course, this element of group work is always troubling for teachers and for group members: what to do when one of the group evades responsibility for the work the group is committed to. In Chapter 5, I'll talk more specifically about how to evaluate groups and the individuals within them. But in this class, and in general with groups, the reflection statement on group work written by each student and the final letter I enclose in students' portfolios are methods of documenting and reinforcing the importance of the small group to the work of the class. My final letter to Stewart included a comment about his poor performance with his group that had been signaled by his absence.

When I look back at these writers in the group, I can say that they all learned something from their experience with one another and with me. Over the next year, Marcia became a confident, skilled writer with a clear, strong voice and a sense of direction in her writing. I discovered her developing abilities when she was my student again three semesters later in a course I taught for teacher certification majors.

At semester's end, Adrian remained hesitant as a writer, but she had begun to seek more help from Shelby and Marcia, and they, because they were becoming confident of their own writing, began to give help more freely. Although she ended the class with some of the sentence and organizational problems she began with, she knew more quickly how to resolve them, and her final journal reflection speaks of her group as the most important factor in making her a better writer.

Shelby was still quiet as the class finished, but he had become more forthcoming with the young women about their writing decisions and more assertive about his own discoveries in what he was writing and reading. He wrote a final comment on his last paper that said, "I feel like a writer. I know I can do it now."

And Stewart? He turned in a short, unreflective portfolio, apologizing for it in his reflective last essay that commented on the semester and on his body of work, and smilingly moved on, I hope, to the art classes he loved. His work in the group hadn't seemed to have helped him much and had even impeded Shelby for some time from developing his own strong writer's voice and from being a good group member. But Stewart was an affable young man and a competent, although reluctant, writer who just wasn't quite ready for the demands of his writing class. My final comment to him said something to that effect.

What Their Teacher Learned

Diversity is a strength. This sentence is almost a classroom cliché. Group work is supposed to value and use the opinions of the various people who make up the group, and students in a group, whether it's a whole classroom or a small group inside it, learn to see how the different backgrounds, experiences, skills, and purposes among them account for varying interpretations and opinions about what they read and write. Still, teachers are tempted—in great measure because of the pressures of time and energy—to see only the unit rather than the bits that make it up. Teachers talk about the class as a whole, make assignments for the group at large, and consider curriculum and lessons in terms of course goals. And, given the way high school and university classrooms are structured, they must view their work in this way. Despite our real belief in the potential that diversity offers for learning, we are hampered in acting on this belief by the need for products to evaluate and for a curriculum that fits into a larger plan for a course of study. Differences among students sometimes become problems to be overcome, rather than facts to be used, in the service of getting the work of the course accomplished.

When I taught the composition course of which the Crows were members, I had lots of experience as a facilitator of groups in the classroom. I knew enough to set up groups well, to give them real work, to value their contribution, and to insist on their own responsibility for one another. But I first saw their diversity as a liability—Adrian not well enough prepared to be a contributing member, especially with regard to responding to the others' writing; Stewart with little interest in the study of literature or the practice of writing—and so I quickly labeled them as a group that would have trouble meshing, being successful. My early comments about the group attest to how much I had programmed them to respond in just the ways I had predicted. The Crows taught me that they could learn to use and value what each of them brought to the group, that their diversity was indeed a strength, and that they could learn these negotiations without intervention from their teacher.

But the Crows also taught me that groups often flourish better with some teacher talk. At the midterm conferences I held with each student during the semester that I taught the Crows, I realized that I should have met with them before. I might have seen how much Shelby needed to see himself as a more active group member; I might have allayed Adrian's anxiety. Marcia and Adrian, who came together for our conference, showed me that meeting with pairs within a group or the group itself (as I have begun to do often since then) helps groups establish a mutual identity as a group and an individual identity as part of a group.

I discovered, too, although it was something I knew well from other evaluations, that the writing that groups did in their group folders could be addressed critically and that my comment to the group rather than to individual writers fostered their work and their planning in future meetings. Following is a piece written by the Falcons in another semester (bird names often remain the same from one semester to another), after a meeting to explore ideas about an essay they had read on identity:

> My group discussed the role taking self. Everyone in the group basically agreed on it. We all decided that everyone has a role model. Everybody looks up to their mom or grandmother or someone in the family. These people have influenced us on the way we dress, act, and our outlook on the world.

I wrote at the bottom: "And who or what are the roles you take? What are the limitations of playing the role? For you—or for your mom/grandmother? Falcons: You need to think harder about your work and your ideas as you write. Think about the objections to your position. Work hard to answer the question you began with."

This group, as you might guess from their examples, was composed of all women, all from North Carolina, two of them cheerleaders in high school, none of them confident of their writing. My comments were designed to push them as a group to challenge their thinking and move together further than any of them might have been willing to do alone. In my institution, it's not unusual to have a class in which two-thirds are women, so there are often all-women groups. With some major exceptions, these groups are more diffident and quicker to move to consensus than are mixed groups. The teacher's comment to a group can help them see how to challenge their thinking about both the issue at hand and how to work in a group.

My intervention in a group's work needs to be timely and pointed. I resist the temptation to sit with a group for long while they work, for fear (proved to be justified on more than one occasion) that I will dominate, get so involved in the conversation that I become the minigroup teacher. But my comments in writing, in conferences, and in the small visits I make to the group as they work are useful if I keep in mind that I'm part of their collaboration as well, not primarily the evaluator of their conversation together.

Finally, the Crows and others continue to teach me that groups need to find their own way. They need to have the freedom to discover one another's interests and backgrounds, what they share and where they differ. They need to go off task as they work so that the social aim—deeply a part of group interaction both in and out of the classroom—has a chance to work. This *socializing* (I'm remembering my teachers in grade school who used this word in deeply offended terms: "Now I'm going to leave the room, but there will be no *socializing* while I'm gone") may seem off the point, but students have to know one another before they can comment to one another. Socializing, in fact, fosters the aim of instruction.

Groups must feel free to talk, but they also need independence in the way they work. Like all the groups in the writing class, the Crows chose their own essay for their presentation, and they decided how and what they would present from the essay. In more general ways in their work, they refined and redesigned what their roles were as group members and how they would handle differences and challenges to their ideas. I try to give groups guidelines for their activity, but I know that groups work best with few and specific guidelines. They must bring their own ideas and approaches to bear on their work and must negotiate them with one another.

In his moving account of the development of literacy *Lives on the Boundary,* Mike Rose (1989) told a story of one such experience in a group he worked with. In an extension program course called the *Learning Line,* Mike worked with a group of people who, for various reasons, could not leave home and took their course with him over the phone. He led a poetry class for residents in several convalescent homes scattered across Los Angeles and taught poems with the kind of sharp images and clear details that his own training had taught him to value. When his students began sending him poems of their own, however, he was surprised and chagrined to see that the poems they sent in were sentimental and strained, with archaic diction and clunky rhymes, "The kind of poems all my schooling had taught me to dismiss," he said (p. 163). As he tried to formulate a plan for responding, for teaching the group how to understand good poetry from sappy, he suddenly realized that the group had provided poems of their own not for critique but for sharing. He said, "They wanted to participate in some fuller way." So he sent to each member not only his selections, but also those of the group and found that they liked both, for different reasons. He was able to talk about feeling and technique in the context of both sets of poems and was rewarded with one student's comment appended to a poem she had written: "Here's a poem like one of the ones Mike sends us" (p. 163).

The lesson of this group for me is that students need to—and will, if they're allowed—direct some of their own work, take it into their own hands. Mike was dismayed by his students' preference for the sentimental, Hallmark card variety of poetry, but his students insisted upon it because they liked it. In their own way, they forced their teacher to take note of their interests and experiences. Once they had their own selected poems given a place, they could bring Mike's poems into relation with theirs. In other words, students needed to name their own situations as they were entering new ones. We all learn best when we can line up our lived experience against experience to be learned. Only in this way can experience, new and old, be tested and used. Mike's students took control, brought their own agendas to the phone line, and so learned something about the poems from one another and from Mike.

Group members need to have their responsibility to one another made explicit. Students are not used to working in productive groups. The students who tell me when I ask about groups that they were always the only ones who worked show how little many students and teachers understand about how to collaborate and cooperate in groups: "My experience with groups is that I'm always the sucker who works. Everybody else reads the paper or pretends to listen and then just watches me write. That's why I've never liked groups. They get the same credit and I do the work."

I remember once when I taught a freshman composition course and began the class by asking students about their feelings about group work since we intended to do a lot of it. One of the students offered a comment very like the preceding one, and soon almost everyone in the class was nodding his or her head and speaking up: "Me too." "I know what you mean." "I wish I didn't feel guilty if I didn't work." And so on. I held up my hand, mock seriously saying, "Don't you think it's amazing that in this entering class of 2,000 students that the registrar managed to group together only the students who were the *only* ones who ever worked in their groups?" They all laughed.

In *The Challenge to Care in Schools,* Nel Noddings (1992) defined *caring* as the ability to be receptive to another—to really listen, see, feel, and consider what another is conveying. Noddings argued that teachers must find ways to attain this relationship in their conversations with students and that students must learn how to care for one another and for themselves in this attentive, nonjudgmental way as well. Dialogue, begun and sustained in small-group conversations, reinforces this attitude of caring that Noddings found so lacking in education. She said, "It [dialogue] connects us to each other and helps maintain caring relations. It also provides us with the knowledge of each other that forms a foundation for response in caring" (p. 23). If teachers and students learned how to listen and speak with care, in Noddings' sense of the term, students would be unlikely to remember themselves as "the only one who worked" in a group.

*   *   *

My teaching life has been a process of learning to teach and model the "ethic of care" Noddings' work describes. I have had to learn to let go—of authority, of myself—a lot more than I was immediately comfortable with doing. I had to learn a new way of teaching. I had to learn to put my belief in the interactive pedagogy of Paulo Freire, the learning theory taught by Lev Vygotsky, and the dynamic nature of interpretation outlined by Louise Rosenblatt into the framework of a classroom whose boundaries seem preset and whose work as a result too often consists almost entirely of teacher talk, discrete assignments, and individualized assessment.

Andrea Lunsford, a pioneering researcher in collaborative writing, wrote of how her own deeply held ideas about how learning happens, ideas promoted by academic training and by the culture itself, altered as she did exhaustive research into writers' processes and strategies. These ingrained ideas, what Lunsford called the *storehouse* and the *garret*, assume that knowledge resides either totally outside the learner—in writing centers, in books, in learning materials—or totally inside the learner—waiting to be brought out by a good listener or coach. Both these models are highly visible in our discipline and in the work all teachers do, and the notion of collaboration calls both into question. Lunsford (1991) said, "To my chagrin, I found more and more evidence to challenge my ideas, to challenge both ideas of Storehouses or as Garrets. Not incidentally, the data I amassed mirrored what my students had been telling me for years: not the research they carried out, not their dogged writing of essays, not *me* even, but their work in groups, their collaboration, was the most important and helpful part of their school experience" (pp. 4–6).

Lunsford's research led her to make six claims about collaboration that can help teachers think about why group work is crucial to class-room instruction:

1. *Collaboration aids in problem finding as well as problem solving.* This insight comes from Ann Berthoff's work, which argues that learning occurs best when students learn to *problematize* their thinking; that is, invent questions as well as answers.[2]

2. *Collaboration aids in learning abstractions.* It aids in learning the relationship between abstractions and their concrete examples as well.

3. *Collaboration aids in transfer and assimilation; it fosters interdisciplinary thinking.*

4. *Collaboration leads not only to sharper, more critical thinking, but to deeper understanding of others.* To understand others more deeply is to sharpen critical thinking.

5. *Collaboration leads to higher achievement in general.*

---

2. See Berthoff's chapter in *The Making of Meaning* (Montclair, NJ: Boynton/Cook, 1981), "Towards a Pedagogy of Knowing," which suggests the role of inquiry in knowledge.

6. *Collaboration fosters excellence.* Especially to the extent that collaboration fosters a sense of responsibility, enthusiasm, and engagement, it nurtures skill and achievement (pp. 4–6).

To change our practices more organically and truthfully in the classroom, and thus to have groups really work in the way they promise to do, teachers must understand and engage critically the theories about learning and literacy that form the basis for much of the advocacy of groups in the classroom. In understanding these roots, we begin the process of connecting to experience and modifying theories to fit the practices we find emerging.

Chapter Two

How Learning Happens

In a graduate seminar I once taught, one graduate student leading her small group asked everybody to pretend to be first graders and invent a game. I was part of her group that night, and I listened in on (and occasionally participated in) the discussion. She asked the group to design our own game that would show the rest of the class how important it is to follow the rules. The four of us got into a first grader's stance almost immediately, and as we invented, I recorded the talk. Here's how the conversation went:

"What do you mean?" (*This comment is directed to the graduate student leader.*) "A game like Duck Duck Goose?"

"Or, how about like School?" (*The leader nods and moves away from our group.*)

"What kind of game is that?"

"You know, you sit on steps and then you get to move up if you get a rock."

"That's 'step up'!"

"No, I think it was called Rock School."

(*The graduate student leader returns to our group, playing her role of first-grade teacher.*)

"Boys and girls, remember you need to invent your *own* game, one that shows how following directions is important."

(*Mock chastened, our group begins again.*)

"So then. Ok. You want to make a new game—"

"Let's make it King and Queen."

"And say if you want to be what kind . . ."

"That's the name of the game!"

"You have to jump on the chair—"

"Just when the teacher is coming in!"

"Yeah, that's a big part of the game. She's got to be gone."

"And jump down and not be caught."
"Ok. *You'd* always be caught."
"You would."
"And you have to say 'pantyhose.'"
"Three times."
"And then you're King."
"Can girls be King?"
"Definitely."

Of course, the playacting was accompanied by much laughter and many digressions not accounted for in this partial transcript. But perhaps you can hear the way these sophisticated graduate students immediately became first graders in their syntax, their interactions, and their attempt to make the group do what the "teacher" had said they should.

The graduate student who gave us our assignment was part of her own small group who, that week, were presenting to the seminar the results of a research study they had conducted on the uses of social speech and play to foster learning. Each student in the group had created an activity, and the first-grade game was one of these. The seminar participants had together studied the work of Lev Vygotsky, the Russian psychologist whose observations about children's behavior have become so important to the study of learning and linguistic development. The project each student group presented in my class attempted to apply and test one or more of Vygotsky's perceptions about learning.

Because they were working in groups while they were studying the way groups worked, all the students in the seminar were highly conscious of the process they followed to come up with ideas, design experiments and observations, and draw conclusions. Because they composed a collaborative paper reporting on their projects, they saw for themselves the way individual ideas get modified and transformed in the social space of the group working together. Not all of them were comfortable with the process of learning to work so consistently in groups. In this chapter, I talk about how the class negotiated the difficulties of collaborative work, and I use examples from lots of other classrooms to show how groups operate to foster the kind of development that Vygotsky and others have shown to be crucial to the way learning happens.

In the preceding play conversation, our "teacher" noted that we performed many of the same operations as those performed by the first graders she had taught and observed in her church day care class. Like them, we began with some games we knew, and we spent a fair amount of time verifying the rules of these games. We had to be reminded to move on to our task, to invent our own game. We began our game with the goal and worked backward. We added to one another's ideas about how the game should be played. We laughed and digressed. We came up with a game we liked. We wanted to play it.

These strategies of moving back and forth, digressing, listening, and playing with possibilities get enacted in countless conversations in and out of classrooms; in fact, they underscore and illustrate Vygotsky's ideas about the way that language and learning happens. Vygotsky's observations and experiments led him to draw premises about behavior that all the experiments of my graduate students demonstrated and that all people use as they interact and learn.

Vygotsky's Premises

Vygotsky's experiments with children in postrevolutionary Russia grew from his reading of the Swiss child psychologist Jean Piaget's study of childhood development that had led Piaget to posit a theory of how mental processes such as perceiving, remembering, and reasoning changed and grew as children matured. Vygotsky was profoundly influenced by Piaget's conclusions, but he found many of them incomplete and undertook to study for himself how human development worked. He began with three assumptions that he took from Piaget's work (1954).

1. Children's thought and language are not deficient adult thought and language but appropriate and useful to their own age and development.
2. Learning and knowing are active, creative processes.
3. Development occurs in stages as children learn how to think about themselves and the world.

Both Vygotsky and his contemporary Piaget began with the idea that children—and adults for that matter—were active in making meaning, that in solving problems they relied on experimentation and experience in creative ways, and that they built on what they already knew or experienced to develop more skill in both language and thought. But Vygotsky and Piaget differed in other respects. The one of most concern here is the way in which Vygotsky recognized, and studied, the effect of others on individual development; that is, the social nature of language and thought that determined learning.

Piaget had posited that language was of two types—*egocentric* and *social*—and that children begin with egocentric speech because it's the type closest to themselves, concerned not with communication but with self-exploration and explanation. Piaget (1954) believed that as children develop, they move to a consideration of the outside world and others and learn the importance of social communication. "To put it quite simply," said Piaget, "we may say that the adult thinks socially, even when he is alone, and that the child under seven thinks egocentrically, even in the society of others" (p. 40). Piaget believed that the course of development moved from inner world to outer world, from egocentrism to socialized behavior.

Vygotsky replicated some of Piaget's experiments with children and came up with a different explanation of development that began, not concluded, with the social. In Piaget's scheme, Vygotsky (1991) said, "socialization is a force that is alien to a child's nature. Socialization occurs when the child's egocentrism is over-ridden" (p. 47). In contrast, Vygotsky believed that from the beginning a child interacts with reality, the outside world, and learns how to manipulate it. She cries; she is fed. He smiles; he is touched. From this social beginning, consciousness—and thought—begin to grow and develop. In other words, Vygotsky showed that the social is from the first the stimulus to the development of language and thinking. Part of this interaction has to do with practical activity, the use of tools and signs, and part of it has to do with interaction with others. But in both cases, the child engages with something outside his- or herself to solve a problem or learn from a new experience. And from this interaction the child develops not only a sense of the world, but also a sense of self.

Vygotsky thus emphasized *context*, the social and cultural connection a child makes with the world around him or her, and consequently he underscored the crucial role that the outside world plays in fostering individual development. The small conversation among seminar participants pretending to be first graders demonstrates how social connection works to help individuals solve problems, mediate disagreements, and reach goals. Even when children, and adults, are alone, they use strategies that groups use to solve problems for themselves. They operate with what Vygotsky called *inner speech,* an internal talk he defined as thought saturated with sense that operates just below the level of conscious awareness and that is at once individual and social. When I talk to students about inner speech, I make the definition tangible by pointing to a place on my neck just below my earlobe and telling them that this is where inner speech resides. I want them to recognize that inner speech is a mediating space, somewhere between brain and tongue, between thinking and sensing, between speech and idea.

Children solve problems, or develop thinking strategies, as they play with tools and ideas. Vygotsky's research shows clearly that children decide on goals, think through plans, develop alternatives, and reach decisions by working through, or playing with, various routes. Following is an example of one of the experiments Vygotsky's (1978) group of researchers carried out. The actions the researcher noted are in parentheses.

> A four and a half-year old girl was asked to get candy from a cupboard with a stool and a stick as possible tools. (Stands on a stool, quietly looking, feeling along a shelf with stick.) "On the stool." (Glances at experimenter. Puts stick in other hand.) "Is that really the candy?" (Hesitates.) "I can get it from that other stool, stand and get it." (Gets second stool.) "No, that doesn't get it. I could use the stick." (Takes stick, knocks at the candy.) "It will move now." "It moved, I couldn't get it with the stool, but the—, but the stick worked." (p. 25)

Vygotsky noted the crucial importance of speech in helping this child solve the problem. She played with various ideas about how to reach her goal, and her playing involved talking to herself and to the experimenter. Although the researcher didn't respond, the child used the other person's presence to confirm or test her idea about how to solve her problem with the candy.

The story at the beginning of the chapter shows how play works in group situations. The goal was to create a game. The "children" played with alternatives, building on those that seemed to get them close to the game's plan and rejecting those that didn't work well. They "used" one another not only to test ideas and then move quickly to alternatives when they got responses, but also to build on others' responses to move their own ideas farther along.

Vygotsky and Group Work

It's no doubt already clear that Vygotsky's observations and theories about learning processes have lots of implications for teachers and for the uses of group work in the classroom. Arthur Applebee's (1996) work on curricular change in education in *Curriculum as Conversation* can help us see how understanding processes—or theories—might affect teachers' work. He noted that curricular structure "is likely to reflect current understandings of the natural processes of thought and language" that are required to participate in the particular curricular domain. What teachers believe about how learners learn is inevitably, even if unconsciously, translated into their practices. Once teachers understand how processes work, they begin to find ways to remake their curriculum, to create new practices and transform older ones.

Applebee used writing instruction as an example of how understandings about processes affect teaching and learning. In the 1970s, the work of Janet Emig, Peter Elbow, Mina Shaughnessy, and others offered new ways of seeing how the writing process worked. When teachers began to conceive of writing as a set of processes that involved generating ideas, drafting, revising, editing, and sharing (or any number of terms for the way writing moves from idea to product), "they began to reorganize classroom activities around their understanding of these processes" (Applebee, 1996, pp. 111–12). Some of the activities that entered the curriculum were new; others were familiar but reorchestrated in the service of the new image of what writers do. According to Applebee, "These procedures in effect reorganized what students did when they wrote in a number of supporting activities that reflected our best understanding of natural processes of thought and language" (p. 112). Eventually, Applebee argued, textbooks and typical classroom patterns began to reflect this reorganization.

Vygotsky's ideas reveal the inescapably social—both communal and interactive—elements crucial to the learning process, and teachers' understanding of these ideas can initiate new and transformed activities that utilize more consciously the social and the collaborative. When teachers design curriculum and activities with groups in mind, they make room for the kind of development of thought and language that Vygotsky showed to be central to learning. They set in motion new processes and new traditions, traditions, as Applebee said, that concern more than just concepts and the vocabulary associated with them, but "characteristic ways of reaching consensus and expressing disagreement, of formulating arguments and providing evidence, as well as characteristic genres for organizing thought and conversational action" (p. 9). The opposite is also true. When teachers limit the social aspects of the classroom—as many do for various reasons—they limit students' abilities to learn. In later sections of this book, I discuss why Vygotsky's ideas about the social nature of learning are so hard to implement in classrooms, and I describe specific strategies for teachers to use to make group work an organic, ongoing, and meaningful part of their course plans and their activities.

An early proponent of group work, Kenneth Bruffee, traced the history of collaborative learning in groups in his famous 1984 essay "Collaboration and the Conversation of Mankind." Bruffee outlined the beginnings of collaborative groups in the college classroom growing out of the open-admissions policies in the late 1960s and early 1970s that flooded classrooms with students who had been poorly prepared to adapt to traditional or "normal" conventions of the college classrooms. Attempting to give students an alternative to traditional classroom teaching, colleges turned to peer tutoring and to peer groups within the classroom itself. In a typical peer group session, one that will strike familiar chords with teachers using group work now, students in the group would analyze the structure of a paper, paraphrase it, and comment on its successes and what might be done to improve it. Or a teacher would set a task with a piece of literature or an idea, and small groups would work together to provide a response, attempting a tentative consensus that allowed the group to report to the class or to the teacher, who evaluated the results.

This kind of collaborative group "harnessed the powerful educative force of peer influence that had been—and largely still is—ignored and hence wasted by traditional forms of education" (p. 638). Students learn from peers because they value peers' opinions and are influenced by them in ways that they're not influenced by teachers. And, of course, the pressure of both the grade and the articulation of an idea to a powerful authority figure is diminished when the writer or the responder is talking to others who are in similarly powerless positions in the classroom.

I've often told students that one reason I like them to write for one another and to show one another their work is that they'll write and turn in things to me that they'd never give to someone they cared about, like their fellow students. We all laugh when I say this, but the point is made: students do care about one another and one another's opinions in ways that they can't care about their teacher, whose reactions are limited by his or her more limited role in their lives. As their evaluator, he or she's supposed to find what's wrong or missing. Their fellow students are in other roles—friends, colleagues, cohorts—and they share a context that makes their opinions matter in ways that reach beyond the individual paper or presentation. While these descriptions of the teacher/evaluator and the student/fellow sufferer may not be true in actual classroom life, students often believe them to be, and their belief about these roles inevitably affects their behavior.

Bruffee said that teachers in the early days of the writing-process movement thought of collaborative learning as distinguished from traditional classroom practices not by *what* people learned as much as *how* they learned it. But teachers limited the work, and consequently the effect, of small-group work by inserting it only occasionally into traditional discussion-lecture formats, by confining group tasks to peer revision of student drafts, or by placing collaborative learning groups within a writing center where small-group tutoring took place. These limitations suggested to teachers and to their students that small groups were primarily add-on features to basic classroom instruction and that these activities were designed as a help and courtesy to students who couldn't learn well in more traditional, individualized ways.

Bruffee's article is important because it describes the uses of collaboration in far more philosophical and conceptual ways than the "peer influence" argument that led to peer tutoring and peer response writing groups in the early days of the writing-process movement. Bruffee eventually began to draw the tentative conclusion that what people learn does get changed by how they learn it. Thought—learning and knowing—in fact, is created—not just replicated—by social interaction. This makes group work become a method much more far reaching than its benefit to the underprepared or to the young people controlled by peer influence. Like Vygotsky's work, Bruffee's underscored the centrality of the social, and the collaborative, in learning.

Vygotsky and the Teacher

To see the role of the group as necessary to learning is not to see the role of the teacher diminished or subverted. Vygotsky's ideas suggest that the teacher's function, as well as peers', is crucial in students' development. A skilled teacher not only introduces a learner to new experience, but also fosters the connections and transformations that the new experience provokes by talk, challenge, and reinforcement—all activities that move the learner beyond what he or she might be able to consider alone. The *zone of proximal development* is Vygotsky's term for the place where the actual (what the learner can do) moves toward the possible (what the teacher or other partner helps the learner conceive). Teachers who see themselves and their students in this dynamic way begin to think of new ways of asking questions, responding to writing, designing assignments, and nurturing student talk.

I watch a teacher in her writing class. She is working in one large group, all of them in a circle, preparing them for the small-group work of responding to one another's writing. She talks to them about her experience as a graduate student getting help and commentary from her fellow teacher, as she shows her colleague her dissertation prospectus. "I knew it was a draft," she tells her class, "but I somehow didn't want her to tell me anything that would make me change it. There was some kind of sense that she didn't know any better than I did what should go in and what should be crossed out." She laughs. "Do you all feel like that?" One student, a male returning student, nods. "I want to tell you you're the teacher. You should tell me what's wrong, correct it." They begin a conversation, then, about what a writer should want from a reader, or a teacher, or an editor. They don't all agree. But they have begun to see the texts they hold in their hands in a different way, and their conversation when they move into small groups of three or four shows that the teacher's opening comment has let them find a new "zone," a place they might not have reached as quickly without that discussion, where they see their responsibilities as responders and their opportunities as writers.

In another book on teaching and learning, *An Unquiet Pedagogy* (Kutz and Roskelly, 1991), I told the story of Carrie, my then two-year-old niece, confronting for the first time an elephant at the circus where I had taken her. Carrie had a category for a four-legged shaggy lumbering creature that was filled by my dog, whom she called "gaga."

When she saw the elephant lumbering along in the ring fairly far from her, she excitedly called out, "Gaga, gaga, gaga." Only as he came closer did she look at me, puzzled. She knew there was something wrong with her category. "BIG gaga," she decided. When I told this story in that book, I highlighted what I saw as Carrie's reach into the zone of proximal development, her ability to line up old experience against new and find similarity and difference. She knew she needed something else, and size seemed like a good distinguishing feature.

What I didn't see clearly then was the role I played as the teacher in that scene. I remember that I laughed and gave her the name *elephant* and talked about how he looked like a dog from far away and how funny he was and how smart she was for seeing how much they were alike. I would now stress the importance of the social in that learning scene. I see Carrie's desire to communicate to herself and to me the new experience she was having, her delight in finding connections and seeing differences, and her ability to move to a new communicative moment as she understood and applied elements of her new and old categories of "gaga" and "elephant."

Humans don't confront reality directly—even big elephants. They find the reality of what they experience through language and other symbol systems. As Karen Burke LeFevre (1987) argued in her book, *Invention as a Social Act*, humans don't invent the language they use, "they absorb it from others in a culture. Language is thus a dialectic between the individual and social realms" (p. ix). Carrie's language allowed her to name reality and name the elements that didn't fit the reality her language could name. My language worked to move Carrie's developing language along, to give her not merely a new name but a new category to think with. At the circus, in church, fixing lunch, "teachers" and "students" are always transforming both their language and their strategies for making sense of what they experience.

Yet sometimes teachers fear or mistrust group work for the way in which it appears to undermine or lessen the teacher's role or the way it might lessen actual learning. "What if they come up with the wrong conclusion?" a teacher asked me once when we were talking about how to use small groups in her large political science lecture class. She was worried that without good information, carefully drawn inferences, and clearly labeled conclusions—all elements of the excellent lecture-discussion classes she led—students would not be able to master the course material and understand the field concepts. And it's true that when students move into groups to discuss texts or ideas, they may come up with conclusions other than what the teacher might have had in mind.

In a composition class I once observed, the teacher told me she was interested in having students "relate, qualify, question" when they

Figure 2–1   Group working on "Big Things": Students' positions

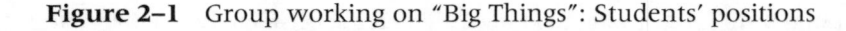

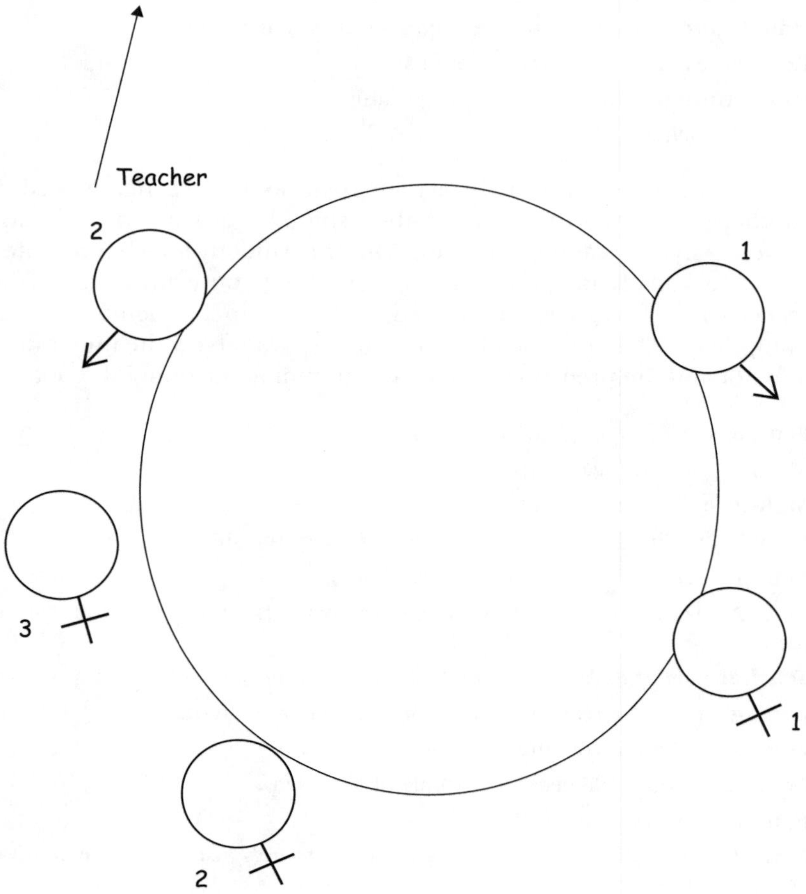

Teacher

2

1

3

1

2

worked on drafts of their essays, not deal with correctness but with response. But in the first few minutes of their discussion, the small group I was sitting with (see Figure 2–1) changed the teacher's plan to deal with points they wanted to consider first when she came over to talk to them:

Teacher (*looking at a draft*): Any suggestions for how to make this more persuasive?

Male Student 1: Look at the comma stuff.

Teacher: And think about all the introductory phrases—good. You guys are good with this comma stuff. (*She reads a phrase aloud.*)

Male Student 2: I want to know the difference between *true* and *very true*.

Female Student 1: He uses *you*. Is that good?

Male Student 2: That sentence seems a little strange to me.

Teacher: Suggestions? praise? commas?

Male Student 2: It's a very true beginning.

(*They all laugh.*)

The students continued on their own, as the teacher moved to another group, and their conversation shifted to matters of audience, as well as style and appropriateness. They read quietly for a few minutes, then they called out to the teacher, "Anything you want us to look at especially?" The teacher responded, "Be open to comments. Take big things first." The draft they began to discuss was about the importance of work and the problems people face in finding meaningful work.

Female 1: George is right. The tone is—

Male 1: Non-outrage.

Male 2: It gives an alternative idea.

Female 2: What if an English teacher said it was too short?

Male 1: Elaborate—put more details. It's all general.

Male 2 (*the writer*): Give an example of the plan? How much do you want to read?

Teacher (*coming back into the conversation*): What more do you want to know?

Female 1: If there really is such a thing, if there are alternatives.

Female 2: I'm not convinced.

Female 1: You could give an example of your dad.

Female 2: You might could mention—

Male 1: Seems like if he was listing reasons—there's just something about it. Too general.

Female 1: But we've read this direct, general kind of approach before.

Male 1: Add one or two sentences to say what you're going to say . . .

Female 3: From specific to general?

Male 1: I think I'd use that first sentence and then go into something personal or some example.

Male 2: What's my audience?

Female 3: People who are working.

Male 1: Anybody concerned with these issues of work.

Notice that the students moved back and forth between matters of intention and form, between what would satisfy them as readers and what they believed to be appropriate structures for the essay itself.

They were taking the "big things," as the teacher asked them to, but not necessarily first. In fact, they demonstrated exactly how embedded form and content are in each other, something the teacher had pointed out to them in earlier discussions. In other words, they took a path other than the one the teacher thought out beforehand in her planning for the group, but in their own way they were finding strategies for improving the writing they were all working on, in both argument and style.

Race and Gender and the Group

Groups working together make conscious and explicit the operations of the thinking mind, lining up what's known against what's unknown, making categories, deciding on paths, revising plans, discovering evidence, and considering opinions. And, to the extent that groups are composed of diverse individuals—people whose social and cultural backgrounds vary, whose race and sex and ethnicity are not the same— groups work to foster the goals of any good multicultural curriculum: opening the minds of students to a variety of approaches and ideas.

In the preceding small-group conversation, the men and women in the group negotiated their differences as they read, and although the females remained quiet early in the conversation, they began to offer both suggestions and responses as the conversation warmed up. Deborah Tannen's (1994) work on gender and language provides, as she said, "a rich site for analyzing how power and solidarity are created in discourse" (p. 45). The interactions between males and females in groups are linguistically complex, Tannen argued, but they reveal how often females are quiet in male groups or how often males talk and females listen or limit themselves to making encouraging comments to help males continue to talk. If you look carefully at the preceding conversation, you'll see that the females in the group did encourage and offer suggestions rather than simply point to problems: "You could put in the example of your dad." Or they clarified and softened, "[Do you mean] general to specific?" But in this group, females were active in helping set the agenda for the group. At one point later in the group meeting, two students were talking and one male (the writer) interrupted to make his point. The second woman stopped him with a sentence: "You're talking over the top of her." He was clearly surprised, but not offended. He asked the woman whom he'd interrupted to continue.

Let's examine one more example of a group in action before we look at some strategies for implementing Vygotsky's ideas with small groups in the classroom. In one freshman writing class I taught, two groups got into a heated discussion about affirmative action after reading David Guterson's (1994) novel *Snow Falling on Cedars*. The novel concerns the effects of World War II and Japanese internment camps on a small town in the Northwest. (Discrimination against Asian Americans in World War II, a key plot element in the novel, led the students to their own contemporary connection with affirmative action.) In the Bluebirds group, Raymond rather loudly claimed that affirmative action was unnecessary in this post–Civil Rights Era. He talked about jobs and housing and education, all opportunities "everybody has" now. The others in his group, four young women, all, like him, from North Carolina, were quiet. But the Cardinals sat next to the Bluebirds, and Charlene, sitting right behind Raymond, spoke up. "Where did you go to school?" she asked.

"In Charlotte," he looked around, surprised to hear from another bird group.

"Well, I went to school in eastern North Carolina. My school was almost all black. And let me tell you there weren't many books in the library or after-school trips. They didn't even bring in job counselors for the seniors."

Raymond was clearly not expecting comment from someone in another group, and from an African American student. He listened and then said, "Well, that's wrong."

Charlene wasn't finished. "So that's maybe why affirmative action is still something we need. Not everybody gets the same chance."

"Yes," one of Charlene's group added, "and especially if you're black."

Raymond and the rest of the Bluebirds went on to discuss other issues in the novel. But the next day, Raymond asked me if he could address the class. The groups had already made their small circles, and they turned toward him as he stood by the Bluebirds group. He wanted, he said, to talk about what he had learned from Charlene the day before: "I guess I was thinking my experience in high school is pretty typical of everybody's in this class. And that's not true."

I'm not sure if Raymond changed his idea about the need for affirmative action as a result of the exchange with the Cardinals, but he did rethink his own first, confident statement. He was learning to use the experience of someone else to help him think about the positions he held. And his need to talk to the class about what he had learned showed how he both valued and trusted the classroom groups. Especially when classrooms confront issues of race, students need to value their fellow students and trust them. The small group, as we've begun to see, nurtures just this kind of belief and trust.

The next two chapters deal more directly with issues of race and gender as they affect the way individuals work within their groups, but even in the preceding two examples, it's clear that groups themselves can discover ways to negotiate these issues as they arise. The teachers in both cases set in motion the method for such negotiation to occur by the way they designed their classrooms to make groups function successfully.

Practices from Theories

Real practices grow from the implications teachers take from Vygotsky's work on the process of learning and the potential of the social group. Many teachers use some of these practices already, and they support Vygotsky's central understandings about how learners learn, including the zone of proximal development, the interrelationship between social speech and inner speech, and the importance of play.

The Zone of Proximal Development

Vygotsky defined the *zone of proximal development* as the distance between actual development and the level of potential development determined through problem solving, often with more-capable peers. The way that children interact with others as they play and work together illustrates learning development, models it, and strengthens it. Vygotsky noted that one flaw in most testing programs (remember that he was writing long before the plethora of standardized tests that children and adults are now subjected to throughout their school lives) lies in the false assumption that only the things that children can do on their own indicate mental abilities. So, if teachers or others provide leading questions as they test children, or if they demonstrate how a problem can be solved and the child then solves it, or if a child completes a problem in collaboration with other children, the solution is not regarded as indicative of the child's mental development. Vygotsky (1978) argued that individualized testing of this sort does not reveal the complete range of ability or development of a thinker: "What children can do with the assistance of others might be in some sense even more indicative of their mental development than what they can do alone" (p. 85).

This statement suggests that schools need to find ways to test how much students are learning, how much they're developing cognitive strategies, by asking them to solve problems in groups, by giving them prompts, by providing examples. If teachers believe that learning develops socially, we need to assess students in social situations. Many of us remember the old report card evaluation from our elementary school days: "Works and plays well with others." Schools need to include this statement again as part of their assessment measures, and not just in the primary grades. "Works and plays well with others." "Learns from others." "Teaches others." "Listens to others." These skills, which are the skills that come from an application of Vygotsky's zone of proximal development, support and extend the other skills—of analysis, memorization, correctness, and generalizing—that report cards and tests now measure.

One of my students in a course that prepares teachers to teach noted how his own development had been strengthened by his work in a small group whose task was to explore several articles on journal keeping for the whole class:

> I guess my role in the group was to set the foundation for the discussion. I began by outlining the dichotomies my own author noted as well as what some of the other authors mentioned. The other group members took it from there. I think I also helped them understand how public and private writing go together. I made them see that in almost every form of writing we do, our personal feelings are an underlying factor.

This student saw himself as the group member who fostered the proximal development of the others in his group. I had asked all the students to write about their contribution to the work of their groups, but this student continued by drawing conclusions about how to teach writing:

> As we talked in our group, I learned what I felt about the role of feelings in writing instruction. Often we cloak or disguise these feelings in public discourse because that is what we have been taught to do. We sorted out how the journal is useful because our feelings do play a part, and so do our personal insights and attitudes.

A first-year student wrote of her contribution to her group in this way, illustrating how the "zone" became someplace where the group as a whole negotiated throughout the semester:

Me as a Part of My Group

> I think I'm the one who'll say anything. Even if I know it's wrong, just for the sake of working through why it's wrong.
>
> I think I work in my group a lot like I have in my journal. I work through things with them. I come with certain ideas that help in the process, but a lot of it is self-discovery through examination.
>
> I'm not really sure how I've helped the others in the group if I have at all (personally) but I think our group as a whole, has made everyone in our group at *least* a little different than they were on the first day of class—and I know I'm part of that.

This beginning writing student saw how her own strategies as a writer were replayed in her work in the group. Her journal writing where she "works through things" was like her group discussion where she worked through things again "with them." She realized that she had changed and been changed by the group, and she saw this as a positive outcome in the class. Her group had become a zone of proximal development itself, a place where everybody had ended up "a little different." She knew she had learned to work and play well with others.

The uses of mixed groups in finding the zone. How do groups provide a spot where the zone of proximal development can flourish? What are some ways to conceive of the group, in its creation and implementation, to help students become conscious of how their own development is enhanced by the presence of others?

One of the rationales for *homogeneous* or *tracked* groups—that is, learners grouped in terms of their ability as demonstrated on standardized tests—is that those who are more able students will be held back by those who are less able. And, as if not to sound too elitist about it, proponents of such grouping note that the students who are less able will likely become frustrated and less and less connected to the work of the group the more they recognize their own limitations. Nel Noddings (1992) called this position "a spurious equality," a design that in practice prevents many students from achieving any kind of success. "We strive to place everyone in the higher tracks instead of attacking the hierarchy," she said (p. 41). Noddings felt that the hierarchy, which keeps people "in their place," is what teachers need to fight.

While there may be benefits to homogeneous groups (often benefits that accrue primarily to the system itself to keep it functioning in a status quo hierarchy), the benefits of mixed-ability, or mixed-potential, grouping are much more convincing than arguments for tracked groups once Vygotsky's premises about proximal development are taken into account. The comments from students cited previously demonstrate how students learn to see themselves as one among many, as part of something larger, as both learner and teacher in the group they're part of. Following is one student's (Theresa's) small ethnographic look at her group, her description of each group member:

> *Ethan:* [He] helped me be vocal. The first time we really talked was when we were planning our presentation. From that day on we've been questioning each other on almost everything. He's really been a great influence on me.
>
> *Leslie:* She has a very definite style and it isn't like mine at all. She has shown me a whole different side of so many things.
>
> *Stephanie:* She has so many great ideas she seems to want to work through but she doesn't have the time. I think she has shown me the will of Job in getting through this semester and everything that's happened around her.

Jeff: He was in the class Stephanie and I shared. He disliked it as much as I did. He's just so good. He always has things done early and is such a good example. He really gets into a subject and doesn't go on till it's done in his mind. He's shown me a lot about what I should put into my work.

Theresa commented about what she had learned from each member of her group, recognizing their individual strengths and how these strengths had taught her something about herself or her own writing. The previous paragraph "Me as a Part of My Group" came from Theresa, too, a final comment about how she contributed to her group. As she reflected, Theresa noted diversity (her style "isn't like mine at all"); how actual meets potential development ("He's shown me a lot about what I should put into my work"); and caring and accommodation ("She has shown me the will of Job"). The zone of proximal development works through this process of teaching and learning, speaking and listening, assimilating and offering. Theresa underscored that both men and women had voice in the group; that they all seemed to have found a place.

When groups work as well as the one Theresa was part of, those who know more help those who know less. Ethan questioned Theresa; she learned how to question him. When classrooms create small groups more or less randomly rather than with skills or personality attributes in mind—who's quiet or talkative, who's a good or bad editor, for example—they consciously do as Noddings suggested, attack the hierarchy that prevents students from succeeding in school. The zone has a chance to operate, to improve both the skills of literacy and the human skills of caring. Groups, when they're well prepared for and nurtured in curricular agendas, will teach talkers to listen and good writers to read, as well as teach quiet listeners to speak and insecure writers to be heard. And groups allow teachers to understand the importance of "Works and plays well with others."

Given what's already been said about gender roles, there are good reasons to create groups composed of both males and females. As David and Myra Sadker (1994) pointed out in their book, early proponents of "mixed education" encountered claims from opponents that because boys and girls were headed for different destinies, they should be educated separately "for their distinct life paths" (p. 18). Offering girls and boys identical lessons would do little to encourage womanly interest and skill in domestic activities, these early-twentieth-century educators commented. Notice that it's assumed that these "identical lessons" would mean "boys' lessons"—the subjects of math and science, of logic and Latin. Identical lessons would never include the women's work of domestic activities. On the other side of the argument, advocates of coeducation in those early days argued first that the "presence of girls would refine boys' rough behavior" and second that girls with better educations would make more successful mothers (p. 20).

Observations in my own classes of mixed- and single-sex small groups suggest mixed results. Single-sex male groups often have difficulty interacting with one another in ways that go beyond accomplishing the task set for the group. They are less likely to go off task; they complete assignments quickly, often superficially, and then lapse into silence or occasional commentary. In contrast, women who work together often seem to thrive in single-sex groups. They report that they've become friends; they get enthusiastic; they solve problems together. These groups often take more time to complete tasks than do either male-only or mixed groups. When males and females are mixed, males are often the dominant voices, or the females in the group encourage them to be drawn into the conversation, sometimes to the detriment of other females. If you look back at the previous snippet of group conversation in which the group was discussing one writer's paper, you can see the female striving to include the male in the task and the male allowing himself to be included.

Gender-mixed groups can provide males the opportunity they need for accommodation (remember Raymond's change of position and statement to his group) and assimilation (incorporation of other views into their own). Such groups can provide females with the opportunity to exercise leadership in a forum where they are used to ceding it; that is, when there are males to take the lead. Both the young woman who reminded her fellow group member that he was interrupting the woman who was speaking, and Theresa, who saw herself as a powerful contributor to her group even when she recognized that the two male group members had skills she might not possess to the same degree, asserted their authority in their groups.

As with gender, I have more to say in other chapters about mixed racial groups in the classroom. The benefits just mentioned—listening to experiences and opinions that can transform a person's own opinions, learning to be a speaker or a listener in forums where the student is accustomed to the opposite role, and developing competence and comprehension that comes from encountering other positions—all these are attained by groups mixed by race and ethnicity as well as by gender. One caveat, however: In classrooms where there are few minority students, teachers shouldn't be so desirous of making the mix that they "seed" a minority student in each classroom group. Students need to feel that they are more than representatives of a larger group that their color or ethnicity makes them a symbol of.

The Interrelationship Between Social Speech and Inner Speech

Vygotsky (1978) showed that social speech and inner speech develop together and that the development of one fosters and speeds the growth of the other. Speech itself, as Vygotsky demonstrated, accompanies action and in fact becomes part of the same psychological function as the learner solves problems and tests solutions. "Children solve problems with the help of their speech, as well as their eyes and hands," Vygotsky said (p. 26). In the same way, inner speech and social speech are part of the same complex developmental function, as the learner communicates to someone else and explains to him- or herself. If, as Vygotsky (1991) said, "The primary function of speech is communication, social contact," (p. 34) and if speech helps learners solve problems, then opportunities for social speech—talk designed to explain, get feedback, argue, and speculate—should be a large part of the classroom work. However, social speech is just the speech that often gets short shrift in classes where the main kind of speech that students use is performative: speech designed to "prove" to an evaluator that they have read the material, solved the problem, understood the requirements, and achieved the task.

Obviously, group work encourages social speech, the kind of talk that occurs among peers and where evaluating is less a part of the listener's agenda than the typical teacher-student conversation. Group work also promotes the use of inner speech, speech "designed for oneself" (Vygotsky, 1991, p. 223). Inner speech is in some ways as Vygotsky described it, the opposite of social speech, moving from the external to the internal where "overt speech sublimates into thoughts" (p. 226). As a group member listens to the other members, he or she uses others' speech and his or her own to accommodate new thought and new internal speech. Raymond didn't record his thought processes as he responded to his classmate's criticism of his position on affirmative action, but it's fair to say that he "talked to himself" about both his feeling and hers. His statement to the class the next day became his inner speech made social again. Groups foster this development in great measure because the pressure is less on a student to be right or to stay right in asserting an answer or a position. Groups have the great advantage over the teacher of allowing for the kind of real social speech that can nurture real inner speech.

The uses of groups in developing inner speech and social speech. Next is a bit of a conversation from a first-year writing class that had been reading Mike Rose's (1989) book *Lives on the Boundary*. The instructor, whose class I was observing, asked groups to find a section of the book that they thought particularly important: "Guys. Take charge. Look through the reading for today, agree on a section that you think

Figure 2–2   Group discussing Mike Rose's book: Students' positions

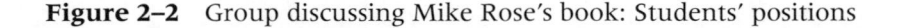

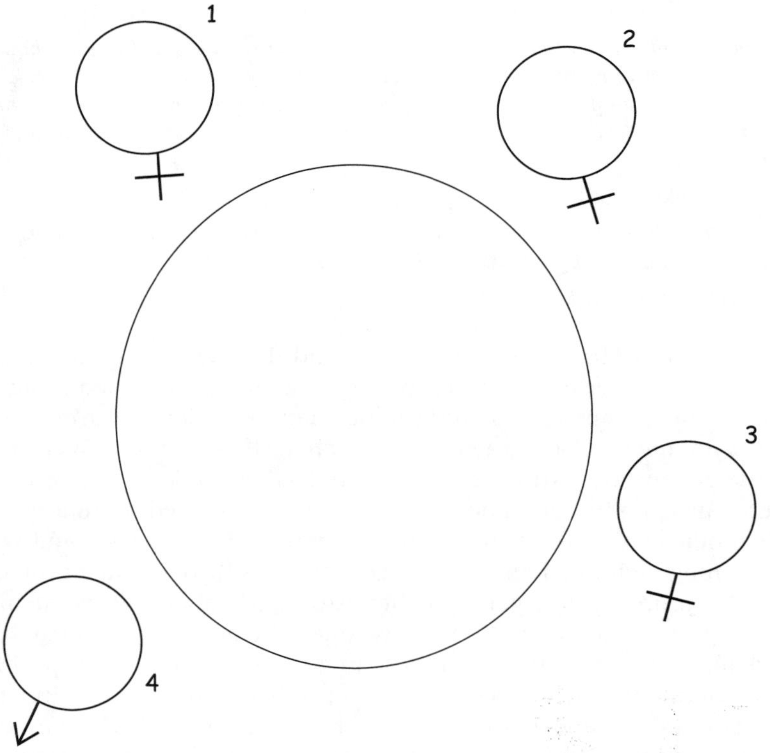

was important and be ready to share with the class why you thought so. I'll give you—oh, six or seven minutes." The class groaned and laughed.

This group was composed of three females and one male (Figure 2–2). One of the women was an African American student. They began by looking at Rose's book, calling out page numbers.

#1: I think he's beginning high school. Remember that time. It was interesting.

#2: It took time to get it.

(*#3 clears her throat; they all look at her. She gives another example from later in the book.*)

#1: Yeah, and then later on, he builds on his reaction—how he learns.

#3: I like that part. He doesn't think when he's in school that—

#1: And then—

(*They all look at book. #1 looks at #4. He looks harder at book. They all read. #1 looks at #4 again. He doesn't look up; stretches.*)

#2: Well, I also like the part about the average guy.

(*#1, 2, and 3 all laugh.*)

#1: And I also like that controlled group. I don't know what else.... Was that all we were supposed to do?

(*#4 moves a little closer into the circle. The teacher warns groups to decide on the scene they will comment on. #1 and 2 talk about the quote they have chosen; #3 looks out at other groups; #4 gets out a survey and moves to the front of the room. #1, 2, and 3 continue talking. They look at book; #1 glances at the teacher. #4 comes back to the group and scoots forward.*)

#1: I also like page 124.

(*#4 opens book and looks at #1. #1 asks #4 a question about his roommate. He responds and then asks what the group has decided. #2 writes a quote from the scene.*)

#4: Will you read that aloud?

This group had a clearly set task, and they spent time looking at various responses to it. But notice how much time was spent reading, offering new examples, and rethinking. Member #4 left the group at one point; member #3 looked away and took herself out of the conversation. These actions are part of the kind of reflective thinking that students were engaging in here, and the tentative, half-formed sentences they used indicate that they knew one another, knew their task, and were combining their inner and outer speech to work through their problem.

You probably note gender issues as well. Member #4 was the male in the group, and he was the one who left the group, responded little, and allowed himself to be drawn in by the three females. His position was dominant, but not because he controlled conversation. But this student both assimilated the ideas of his group members and accommodated himself to them, as he moved away and reflected, returned and commented.

The kind of talk that nurtures the interweaving of social speech and inner speech is at its heart relaxed and in some way equal among the participants. People feel confident enough to share ideas and trusting enough to speculate and rethink *in front of* others. This next bit of taped conversation came from a class of North Carolina Teaching Fellows, a program designed to encourage highly motivated and gifted students to teach in public schools. These students were all seniors, which meant that they were all in the process of student teaching in grades K through 12. They had read Mary Rose O'Reilly's (1993) book *The Peaceable Classroom*, about the ethical and practical dimensions of teaching writing, and they were beginning the process of writing a review of it for a state teachers' journal. There were five group members, all female, two African American (Figure 2–3).

Marian: Well it says in the back that she's Quaker, it also did say in the book that she talked about the fact that she was going to be sending kids to Vietnam

Figure 2–3   Group reviewing Mary Rose O'Reilly's book: North
                Carolina teaching fellows' positions

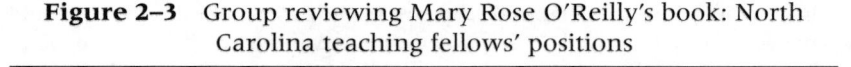

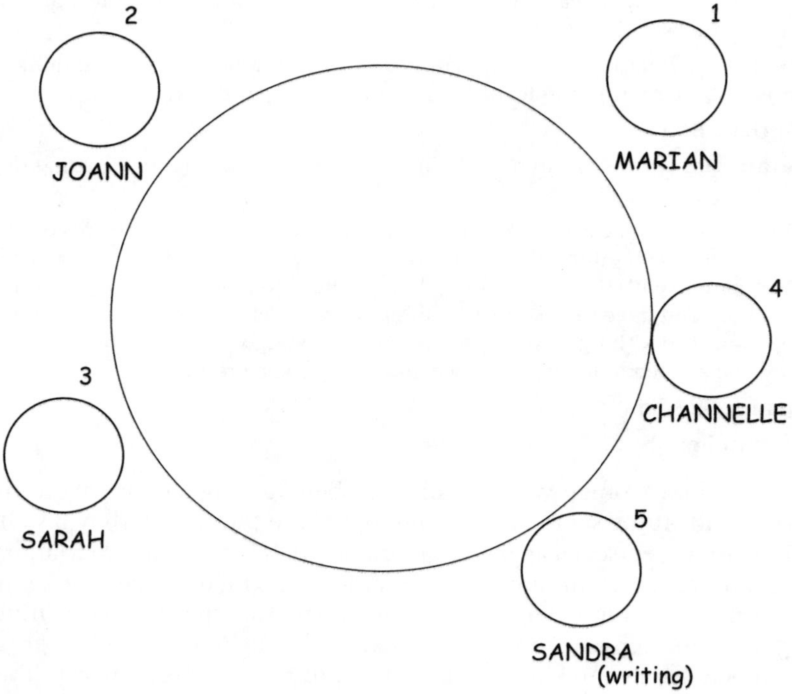

if they flunked.... There was part of it where she goes into that. It's the part
where she starts college—

Joann: Yeah, finish college.

Marian: I mean there are certain things you start catching it and you start to
figure out where she's from. But that was one of my gripes about it, is that she
starts her whole theory before you, before she qualifies who she is and why
she has any validity, why she would know any of this stuff...

Sarah: You have to get into it before you start finding out.

Marian: Where is she coming from? It's like she doesn't give herself a premise
by which you say all right, yeah yeah, I agree that you, okay, now I want to
listen to you. (It's just an) intro with an...all right I have a really high and
mighty goal and that is to teach English so that we stop killing each other so
let's start at the basics and work our way up. She goes from right to left to right
to left and in the middle you kind of sort of pick up who she is and what she
means and it's really hard to join her bandwagon because who are you, what
are you doing and what do you mean, and it's so abstract and it doesn't seem
to fit into concepts of today, you know, the problems of what we're dealing

with. . . . She just sort of starts these peace studies. Which in the sixties would have gone over very well. Peace studies, hey yeah, we're all for peace we're all, you know, against Vietnam and all this. What are you going to do in 1999 though? Forming a peace studies class it doesn't quite seem to apply. So she's kind of, that's—

Joann: Do you think that her, that the difficulty in following, do you think it's because of her writing style, or because of poor organization?

Marian: Both.

Sarah: Or because she, in her attempt at being new and attention getting she's just kind of sporadic . . .

Marian: It's a mixture. One, the organization of the book is not necessarily bad, but it is something that you have to get through the book to see where she's going. So it's the type of thing that you have to really want to get through the book. You have to in some way desire this peaceful classroom and the, you know, peacenik thing. Which I'm kind of, I'm being very critical but it's kinda hard 'cause I liked the idea in a way but it had to be grounded.

Joann: She didn't get you—

Channelle: She didn't hook you first?

The four women were sorting out their varying feelings about this book, and, at the same time, trying to prepare the review they'd write. They used their social agenda to work through both issues. Marian had the most to say at this point; she was the group member who was most critical but also most engaged in the issues. Her speech was as much figuring out her reaction as it was expressing it. And her fellow group members seemed to know that, as they probed her reactions with their questions and allowed her space to sort out her responses. The group continued to talk about O'Reilly's experience in public education and then returned to the topic of peace and warfare.

Marian: . . . and it's the whole thing, that's actually what happened in World War I, that is one of the big poems that they use, or maybe it came after because it's sarcastic about dying in war. And how it is just and good to die for your country well and then after World War I where it didn't make much sense and then you get on to the Vietnam War. So she's criticizing. And you know, it's not a completely unfathomable criticism. I mean we've had this criticism over and over about whether or not it's good. And, but, violence in the classroom or the killing that I think of in the classroom is gang warfare. Not being sent overseas to fight. . . . I'm not sure I completely agree with Bosnia. I'm still not sure what we're doing over there. But that's not what I'm worried about when I walk into these schools. I'm not worried about these kids' being sent to Bosnia. I'm worried about the kid who, when I had to give a test in the special ed class over at Dudley, one kid wouldn't take the test because he couldn't take his eyes off this other kid because the other kid was about to jump him. And I'm sitting there going "Mrs. Reed," you know, having to call the next room's teacher in because I can't even give a test. That's what I want her to address and as of when I was done, she hadn't gotten into that.

Channelle: I think that goes back to what you were talking about, you know, 1960s versus 1999. The kids that we teach today have no real concept of war. You know, maybe father, uncle, brother, cousin went on to Desert Storm but—

Sarah: That was so neat and clean. It wasn't real—

Marian: That's not exactly—

Channelle: And all it was was wearing an American flag. At home Desert Storm was wearing an American flag.

Joann: I'm like you. I'm thinking the only violence they know to counteract peace, you know, is my buddy, my buddy, you know next door just got shot last night. My mom is the one who killed him, you know what, what do you do—

Sarah: Or my mom died.

Joann: Yeah, my mom's the one who died.

The conversation continued quite awhile as the group negotiated and finally came to some clear understandings of what they thought of the book. In part, they rethought their reactions because of the preceding conversation, where they brought their own classroom issues to bear on the central concerns in O'Reilly's text. Their speculations and their associations were sometimes offered in almost tangential ways to what they considered to be O'Reilly's themes and their reactions to them. But the associations became part of the thinking process that connected what they read to who they were as teachers. Inner speech and outer speech—speech for oneself and for others—had merged and mutually reinforced one another in their group work. They ended their conversation and began their review with a more positive assessment of O'Reilly's work than they had begun with—in great measure, I think, because in the process of exploring connections to their own experiences they found them.

The Importance of Play

Vygotsky (1978) pointed out repeatedly the role of play in learning and in cognitive development among children. He defined *play* as creating an imaginary situation with rules and a solution not immediately obtainable—not, significantly, as pleasure. And the importance of this kind of play on a child's development is enormous: "Action in imaginary situations teaches the child to guide her behavior not only by immediate perception of objects or by the situation immediately affecting her but also by the meaning of this situation" (p. 97). In other words, play allows what Jerome Bruner (1986) called the *possible world* to come into being: the world of ideas, not concrete objects.

Learners who play, try out ideas, reject them, create situations, refine them, remake solutions, and redefine problems. They move between actual and possible, and this movement encourages greater and greater facility with both solutions and the language used to express them. Play, then, is purposeful, but it is also—at least in the short run— digressive. The digressions—whether they're tangentially related stories, off-task comments, or discussions of possibilities that fail to work— become playful elements that can contribute to the development of a plan or a piece of writing, or the solution of a problem.

Teachers worry about this kind of play *because* it's digressive. In a time when so much has to be "covered," play feels way too time consuming. This feeling is responsible for the demise of play period in many elementary schools across the United States. Students should always be held to the task at hand, the thinking seems to be, since there is so much sheer *stuff* to do and to remember. But Vygotsky's work demonstrated convincingly how crucial play is to learning. If teachers limit or deny play in favor of the straight path of problem-solution, read-write, question-answer, they constrain students' learning.

Play, because it's governed by rules that the players both create and recognize, is controlled rather than chaotic. In fact, Vygotsky (1978) argued, "A child's greatest self-control occurs in play" (p. 99), and he meant that rule-governed activity insists that players obey the rules they've set up or they lose the pleasure of the play itself. He said, "Play gives a child a new form of desires. It teaches her to desire by relating her desires to a fictitious 'I,' to her role in the game and its rules. In this way a child's greatest achievements are possible in play, achievements that tomorrow will become her basic level of real action and morality" (p. 100). The fear of play as both out of control and too time consuming, then, is misplaced when play is defined in this strategic, conceptual way.

The play group. Groups are tailor made for playing. The group can assign roles, set up rules, act out situations, consider possibilities, and arrive at solutions—and have fun—as they talk together. The group talk that began this chapter illustrates play clearly: the group was *playing* at being children; they engaged in playful activity that led them to the solution they wanted—a game. And they made up rules that let them laugh and imagine. But they were also learning about how important play is in itself. They remembered themselves playing, they saw how creativity is part of learning, and they considered how to make use of this knowledge in the classrooms they were teaching, in both high school and college.

Writing together is a way to make play part of the group's activity. One graduate group, studying Vygotsky and writing a collaborative project on the role of play in group revision of a paper, began its own report this way:

> Considering the high level of attention being given LS Vygotsky in the field of educational research these days, the researchers at the Jane Joe Bill Sam Laboratories for Educational and Scientific Study (better known as JJOBLESS), using convoluted sentence structures and sophisticated reasoning techniques, to wit: "People only research what they expect to find useful, and since people are researching Vygotsky, people must expect to find Vygotsky useful," reasoned that it would be beneficial to conduct an experiment testing one of Vygotsky's theories. . . . Since the primary source of income, headaches, sleeplessness, anxiety, hope, and terror for each of these researchers is teaching college composition, and since their students could provide ~~senseless~~/suitable and ~~coerced~~/willing ~~dupes~~/~~guinea pigs~~/subjects for their experiment, they elected to observe, specifically, the role of play in composition.

The graduate students studying play mimicked play in their own group conversation as well as in their written style of performance. The strike outs, the self-deprecatory opener, the allusion to their own career paths, and the critique of the academic writing of professional researchers point to their own playfulness in composition. They produced a fine study, with clear observations, interesting conclusions, and possible teaching strategies, and their argument, that play in Vygotsky's sense is crucial to revision in peer groups, was wittily enacted in their own work.

If the group itself is an example of play at work, there are also activities, both individual and collaborative, that can foster play in the classroom. Imitation, for example, is a playful strategy that extends and supports learning. Imitation is too often thought of as just a mechanical process, devoid of creativity or real learning. But as Vygotsky (1978) pointed out, a person can imitate only what is in his or her developmental capacity. If a child is having a hard time with an arithmetic problem and the teacher solves it on the blackboard, the child may be able to grasp the procedure and the answer quickly. But no matter how many times a teacher writes a quadratic equation on the blackboard, the child who has never encountered such a math problem won't be able to understand the solution no matter how many times he or she imitates it (p. 88).

Imitation of voice or situation or style helps students understand concepts as well. One assignment I often give my American literature classes is to produce a conversation between two characters caught in a situation: Mary Rowlandson, the Puritan, and her captor Weetamoo, the Wampanoag princess; Harriet Ann Jacobs, the slave woman who wrote her story of captivity, and Harriet Beecher Stowe, who wrote about that story from her own white perspective. I usually give this assignment to groups, so that they can take roles if they want to, so that they can banter, use and reject words, listen to voices, and refer to texts in ways that are productive and playful. They learn from putting two perspectives and two voices together in relationship, and they learn from the several perspectives and voices in their own small group.

One other finding of Vygotsky's about play is the importance of tools to help learners solve problems or gather ideas. The example of the little girl who tried to reach the candy with a stick and a stool in Vygotsky's research study used these tools in various ways as she considered how to reach her goal. Tools reinforce and extend the ability to solve problems. Real objects, tools to draw or build with, can be important to play in groups as they engage in activities together. Groups who draw to help them with projects—graphs, charts, illustrations—engage in hands-on playful activity. If groups make something, design it, bring examples of it, they are using tools to help them make their points clear, their observations solid. The recent emphasis on ethnographic research that searches out small cultures and observes them closely often brings with it an emphasis on artifacts and tools, and these artifacts allow research groups to see more clearly the places and the people they're observing.

One final example of play in action shows how sensitive issues, such as race, can be broached, and understood deeply, in the context of group work and presentation. Gail Griffin teaches English at Kalamazoo College, and her 1995 book *Season of the Witch* is a reflection on teaching, feminism, and the politics of university life. In one section of the book, Griffin wrote of a class studying Zora Neale Hurston's *Their Eyes Were Watching God*. Students formed their own groups, and the three African American students in the class, all women, immediately grouped together and decided to respond to the questions about the novel that were submitted by the class. As Professor Griffin reported, one question that surfaced had to do with "the Porch," the place where characters gather to tell stories or play games. In the novel, the porch becomes a collective voice where issues get worked out and where community gets established. The students in the group began their discussion by saying the following:

> We were surprised that a lot of you didn't understand about the Porch. That's really familiar to all of us from our childhoods, people sitting around on the front porch or the stoop and talking.... That's one way that kids get educated, by listening to adults on the porch. It's how the culture gets passed down (Griffin, 1995, p. 151).

The students told the class that they would discuss the themes Hurston's book brings up as though the three of them were sitting on the Porch. Griffin commented:

> And off they went. One of the trio would pose a question about the novel, using her normal "student" voice. Immediately the trio moved into vociferous argument, in an entirely different voice—full-throated Black. Assertions were made without qualification or concession; opinions were decried outright or enthusiastically embraced. Voices overlapped constantly. The issues were never resolved; the differences were allowed to stand. . . . Instead of talking *about* the Porch, my students had talked *from* the Porch—that is, from a site within the African American tradition. And they had offered us, wittingly or not, another strategy, another metaphor, for discussing ideas (pp. 151–52).

Griffin realized the value of this kind of exercise for what it teaches everyone about how to make arguments and explore ideas, as well as what it teaches about the uniqueness and diversity of experience that can add to the knowledge of the class as a whole. She said, "The African American students had asserted their authority, in the true sense of the word, very clearly: This literature comes from a familiar place to us, they said. We know this, on an entirely different level from the way of knowing we are cultivating together in this classroom. We can help you understand this work" (p. 152).

The students' performance is also a wonderful example of how a small group played together and with their classmates, imitating the styles and stances of the Porch sitters and using their own memories and experiences to lend authority to the imitation. Taking on roles, delivering their small speeches, they helped the class find deeper meaning in Hurston's novel, and they gave voice to their own shared experience.

The Benefits of the Circle

Group work facilitates, and often determines, how learning happens. The group makes talk and knowledge flow in new directions, in a circular path rather than a straight line from teacher to student and back again. This new movement creates more opportunity for talk, and with good talk comes real learning. Because the pressure of performance diminishes when students talk among the three or four others who make up their group, they can converse with greater freedom and less fear than when twenty other students listen and the teacher reacts.

Creativity emerges with freedom. Even among students who tell one another or their teacher, "I'm just not creative," the social and informal nature of the work of the group draws out creativity. Students who write or plan together in groups offer imaginative, eloquent, and surprisingly error-free prose.

Groups allow students to assimilate new ideas, to accommodate others' opinions and experiences, and to develop deeper, fuller perspectives from which to examine what they read and write. This excerpt from a student's journal shows how much she learned about such accommodation from her group:

> I know that being in my group brought out bad traits in me. In my anxiety to have an idea accepted, I caught myself interrupting a couple of times, which is an awful thing to do. Nevertheless, through my positive affirmation of my colleagues' presentation parts, and through my own careful preparation of my assigned piece, I'll make a good contribution.

Another student wrote of the same process:

> Some of us wanted to do a very strict presentation of the entire book covering all of the bases in a highly structured manner. Some of us wanted to throw the material at the audience and incite a round table discussion including the audience. Some of us wanted to do a skit of some sort.... We were able to straighten out the details of the presentation to the satisfaction of those of us who wanted strict order; we were also able to include a class discussion for those of us who wanted to open the doors for potential chaos; we also added an in-class writing in lieu of a skit. Basically, we were able to negotiate and compromise and come up with a presentation that would fit nearly all of the expectations the individual group members had for it.

Finally, maybe most important, groups allow for diverse experiences and ideas to be heard, often experiences and ideas that traditionally have been silenced or ignored in classrooms. Many researchers' work documents how much the learning of African American children especially, although not exclusively, focuses on the social and the interactive, rather than simply on the individualistic. Shirley Brice Heath's (1983) landmark study of learning and culture, *Ways with Words*, examined patterns of literacy that showed how African American children in the small community she studied learned in groups, often, like in *Their Eyes Were Watching God*, by listening and talking on the front porch. Geneva Smitherman's (1977) *Talkin' and Testifyin'* and Lisa Delpit's (1995) *Other People's Children*, both studies of African American children and multicultural teaching, argue in one way or another for the kind of collaboration that group work inspires. Studies of women's language and education—notably Jill McLean Taylor, Carol Gilligan, and Amy Sullivan's (1995) research on race and gender (*Between Voice and Silence*), Maureen Barbieri's (1995) study of adolescent girls (*Sounds from the Heart: Learning to Listen to Girls*), and David and Myra Sadker's (1994) indictment of American classrooms (*Failing at Fairness: How America's Schools Cheat Girls*)—argue how much women thrive when they are encouraged to work collaboratively and cooperatively. For minorities and for women, these studies are emphatic in their claims for collaboration and in their realization of the losses that occur when the circle of group interaction is replaced with the line of teacher-student talk.

Why it's so difficult to foster this kind of conversation, this kind of learning, is part of the subject of Chapter 3, as we look at the challenges faced by teachers and students who attempt to make group work the central part of their work in school.

Chapter Three

The Circle Breaks
Why Groups Fail and
Why They Succeed

Figure 3–1 shows a *For Better or For Worse* comic strip that tells a story that those of us who've worked in groups, or tried to direct groups, know all too well. Groups in school fail often, and markedly, and for lots of reasons. In fact, it seems so hard to make small groups work well—that is, productively—that many teachers abandon them or consign them to any leftover time they may have in a busy class period. Students themselves talk of their struggles as past group members who were "the only one who worked in my group" or whose teachers saw group time as a time to prepare the next day's lesson while the class pretended to do the work the group had been assigned. Both teachers and students struggle with the questions the cartoon poses: why do classes break into groups, and what is supposed to happen in them? In this chapter, I speak of the failures of groups and explore some of the underlying reasons for these failures. Then, using accounts from thoughtful teachers and from successful classroom groups, I describe how and why groups learn to be effective.

Why Groups Fail, Part 1: Dictators in the Group

The comic strip shown in Figure 3–2 dramatizes a tale many students tell of one group member who becomes dominant, who insists on his or her own ideas for the group as a whole, and who makes the experience of working in the group less than pleasant. You can see it in the expression of the young girl in the picture, a kind of frustrated silence that what

56

Figure 3–1   Groups in school often fail

she had offered had been completely ignored by the boy who wrote the dialogue they would present to the class. "I tried to offer my ideas," said one of my students in an early journal entry, "but one group member was so insistent on hers that I just stayed quiet. I know I don't always have the right way, but she was not willing to listen to what I had to say." When one student dominates, the response from other group members is often to capitulate, to "just stay quiet" to get the work done, the project completed, the presentation ready. They suffer, and remain angry or disaffected, but they seldom, in my experience with groups, confront the offender.

Just as in the classroom at large, students generally prefer to remain quiet in the face of a controlling presence, whether it's the teacher or one or two students who always have their hands up, who always respond to the question. If asked about their silence in the large classroom discussion, students say things like "I just don't think as fast on my feet as other people" or "He always has the right idea, and I usually don't." In the small group, though, their silence is accompanied by more frustration. Students in their small group feel more keenly a sense of being shut down or out, in part because of the size of the group and in part because of its designation as theirs rather than the teacher's.

If a group has one person who refuses to listen to the ideas of others and pushes his or her agenda without regard to the ideas of those he or she is working with, the group can't collaborate, can't learn from one another, and can't use individuals' experiences to build shared ones. But often the dominating voice is the person who feels he or she is the only one who works in the group, the only one who cares about the assignment, the only one who's read the material. I can't tell you how many times I've begun a semester with my first-year students by discussing how we'll use groups and they've told me—sometimes to a person—that they were the only people in their high school groups who would actually do the work. "I seemed to always be the one to write what we

Figure 3–2   Group domination by one member

would present," one freshman said, "Everybody else just talked about their weekend. And if I would ask them a question, they'd look at me with blank stares and say something like 'Whatever' and then go back to what they were talking about. Working in groups is a waste of time."

The dominating voice in a small group often believes that he or she is doing the teacher's work, attempting to move the group to do its work efficiently and as the teacher has directed. He or she is often dismayed by the group's reactions and by the teacher's insistence on letting the group work together without much intervention. The problem usually escalates over the lifetime of a classroom group; the more the dominator speaks, the less the other members do. And he or she speaks more and more to make up for their silence, which he or she interprets as a lazy refusal to take on the responsibilities of group activity.

Why Groups Fail, Part 2: Slackers in the Group

In journals, students write about the problem of irresponsible group members much more than they write about overly responsible members (see Figure 3–3). Mary wrote of her experience first as a high school student and then as a college freshman, where she was always the one who did all the work for the group:

> It always seemed like I was the one who always did all of the work and never got the grade I wanted. For example in high school, I was in one English class which based everything on cooperative learning. I was stuck in a group with four other people who were lazy and loved to procrastinate. Whenever we got together in groups, I was the one who had already read the material before class, and I was the one who listened to the teacher's instructions. However, our grade was based on everyone's contribution. Because of this my grade was never where I wanted it to be. The grade was bad, it just didn't reflect my work.

Figure 3–3   Irresponsible group members

The very same experience happened to me last semester in one of my classes! We were asked to conduct a group project where we chose a topic, and gave an oral presentation, first individually, and then as a group. Again, I was the one who conducted the research and organized the project. On the day of the presentation, I received an A for my part but our group grade was a C–! The grade turned out to be a collaboration of our individual grades as a whole. They obviously did terrible!

Another response echoed Mary's:

I suppose that much of my reservation [about collaborative work] stems from bad experiences I've had in the past. When a grade is based on what you *and* someone else does, it makes me a little nervous. Not all the work gets distributed evenly. Not everyone wants to work. So... it does make for a difficult situation when you care about the quality of your work. Especially when you want to learn and others don't. If your colleagues care about their work and have the same goal as you, then you try to work as a team and do your best.

A graduate student, now a teacher himself, wrote about his negative experiences as a group member who had to deal with a slacker in his group:

Most of my pseudo-group experiences occurred when I was an under-graduate. The one I remember best was one in which I was put together with three other people, whose names I never had to learn or really had time to learn. We were given a prompt, which assumed we all had the same degree of knowledge about the text and thus immediately left one group member out of the project because he had not read the assignment. This little problem created a whole host of social issues about how we felt about him and his potential effect on our grade. All I could see from group work in this situation was that other people could bring down my grade rather than help it. When I ask my students about group work, I have found similar experiences among them to be quite common.

For students who see themselves as the only ones willing to work in a small group without the teacher's dominant presence guiding their action, the motivation is almost always connected to the grade or the evaluation the group will receive. And their frustration or annoyance at group members who don't pull their share of the work is almost always connected with how their own evaluation will be affected by the irresponsible group member. "I'll work harder and get the same grade as the slackers," the responsible ones complain. "I'll try really hard but my grade won't reflect it because everybody else won't work." The problem of the grade is deeply embedded in the attitudes of both the workers and the slackers in group work, and in the problems teachers face in making group work an integral part of their classroom practice. Issues of equity—what's fair to students—always center on grades since that's traditionally been the way that education has addressed performance. But fairness in classroom practice has implications far beyond grades: in the way students and teachers respond to one another, hear one another, and use one another. These larger issues of fairness have everything to do with students'—and teachers'—gender, race, and class and cultural backgrounds, and they have implications for alternate ways that groups might be evaluated.

Still, maybe because these larger issues of fairness are so seldom addressed, the problem of who does, or will, take responsibility in the group looms large in the minds of students who classify themselves in their past groups either as slackers or dominators. One student wrote in his journal of his uneasiness with an assignment to write a piece collaboratively:

> Using more than one writer to produce an essay is unfamiliar. Opposing points of view hinder focus. Group work displaces responsibility. I foresee trouble in our upcoming assignment.
>
> Without a distinct focal point a paper loses impact. No two people think alike. Personality conflicts such as: religious beliefs, political stands, and exposure to different experiences scramble a unified thought process. After this breakdown, obtaining a central theme is complicated, if not impossible.
>
> In the words of the great George Forman [sic], "What happened to the fire!" In any group, required to accomplish a task, a leader must rise to the occasion. This responsibility outweighs the other group members' hardship. The imbalance in work effort leaves the leader unrewarded for the extra effort. Thus, motivation for becoming a leader is not present. No motivation equals little, if any, actual work.

This student worried about final performance, about evaluation, and about the conflicts that might arise when differences of opinion emerge and the need to produce work is present. He was clearly concerned about the work of collaborating that lay ahead for him and his group, yet notice how distant his approach to the topic sounds. There is only one "I" in the whole response, even though he clearly had a personal opinion about the matter. His distrust and worry are clear, especially about the issue of responsibility. Although he didn't say *he* might have to be the one to do all the work, he insinuated that if he didn't, likely no one would.

This student saw the need for leadership in the group and the lack of opportunity for leaders to emerge in the collaborative unit of the small group. In his group in class, he demonstrated in his behavior and gesture the conflict he felt. He hung back, literally, pushing his chair away from the rest of his colleagues, three women. He expressed his suspicion of the group process in his body movements, turning away from the conversation by looking down often, reading material while discussion swirled around him. The women in his group expressed worry about him—not worry about the group in general—by their own gestures, which moved them closer to him, had them turning to him, asking him questions, and currying his favor in ways that might allow him to participate.

Gender considerations are always part of group dynamics, even when they're not expressed, and they usually are not. More typically expressed are responses that concern themselves with evaluation, with the way one group member might bear an unfair portion of the work or another might get away with not contributing by allowing his or her partners to do more than their share. Many of the preceding comments, for example, are framed in terms of work, but underlying some of them, as in the case of the worried male student, are issues of gender and concern about the way males and females play roles in their groups. As we'll see, students often have race as underlying reasons for their fears and distrust of small groups as well. And, as with gender, this concern is almost never addressed directly by students or by their teachers.

Why Groups Fail, Part 3: Teachers in the Group

The need for evaluation, and the dominance of grades as the method for evaluation, is part of why teachers feel so conflicted about how they will use groups in the classroom. They voice the same questions as those of their students: What if one student does most of the work? How will I even know that, much less evaluate him or her? How do I give a group grade? Is it fair to give individual grades to a group project? Teachers' negative or ambivalent attitudes about groups—manifested in the way they assign and evaluate them—often cause the group to fail.

When my daughter Kate was in the eighth grade, her social studies teacher became ill and had to leave the classroom for six weeks or so.

He had prepared for his absence with lots of lesson plans and classroom activities, including the work in small groups that his students had been used to doing together. The substitute hired to take his place followed his plans precisely, but she was new to the students and to the school, and the inclusion of group work—which the social studies teacher used nearly every day—no doubt made her feel as if she might lose control. One day Kate came home and reported her group's activities for the day: "The teacher said, 'Ok, everybody get in your groups. And *no talking*. If I hear talking or anybody scraping chairs, we'll never get into groups again'." I asked Kate, "What did you do?" "Well," she shrugged, "we just did the work and whispered to each other."

Get into groups and no talking? Only twelve years old, Kate recognized the foolishness of the demand, but she obligingly, like the rest of her classmates, moved her chair—very quietly—into the circle and proceeded to do her group work by herself.

Another story suggests the reason for Kate's teacher's behavior. I often supervise student teachers during their internships in high school classrooms. One day, I walked into the tenth-grade classroom where a student teacher was teaching a short story. Chairs were all moved into small circles for group work, and students sat in their groups the entire class period while the student teacher discussed the story and asked for comments from the class. After the bell rang to end the period, I met with the student teacher. I was mystified by the arrangement of the desks, I told her. She looked at me and smiled, I hope a little sheepishly. "Well, I knew you liked group work," she said.

Both these examples show how teachers misperceive and thus misuse the small group. It's as though these teachers believe that the chair placement alone means something. Of course, they're right in a sense. The physical arrangement of classrooms *does* send messages about classroom dynamics—where authority is located, how much talk is permitted and what kind, and how interaction occurs. But chairs placed in small circles does not mean that group work goes on, as Kate's experience and mine with the student teacher can attest.

One teacher education student believes the problem with groups rests with the teacher's understanding of his or her goals for group work and his or her reasons for using them: "Normally, I despise group work. Too often, I have been told to form a group, for no other reason than a change of pace or to make up for a lack of effective teaching. Then the group members stare at each other or their books and ask, 'What are we supposed to do?' over and over."

At the beginning of one fall semester's classes, a group of students who would be student teaching the next spring talked to me about the failures of their groups in an educational methods class many of them had just completed. The professor gave few guidelines, never talked with an individual group, didn't hand out written instructions, and gave them no feedback on their work together. The group work also— as much as these students could tell—never figured into the professor's calculation of a final grade. They all felt that *they* were responsible and willing to work but that the teacher hadn't been responsible or willing and so failed the group. To them, she had been using the group to "get them to talk" and to make up for her lack of expertise.

Lack of guidelines, lack of interest, lack of expertise, all these are reasons that students give for the poor way teachers have used groups in their classrooms. Most students I've talked to recognize that groups cannot work well without a teacher's conscious planning and guidance and that many teachers have few ideas about how to plan or guide a group to help it succeed.

Teachers bring up similar complaints. They worry about how much they should intercede. "If I join a group, no one else talks, or else they talk and look at me to verify that they've said the right thing," one teacher told me. Teachers often impose guidelines and discover that the rules have inhibited the group's work. Or they allow groups free rein and discover that, as one student teacher told me, "They get off topic if I don't watch them like a hawk!"

"I don't see that a whole lot gets accomplished in a group," a high school English teacher once remarked to me. "The talkers talk, the silent stay silent."

The Problem with Textbooks

Textbooks for teachers who try to mandate group activity offer little real help for the problems just described. Following is an example of an activity suggested in a textbook on teaching first-year writing (Erickson and Strommer, 1991):

> Small-group methods offer practical alternatives for engaging students in discussion no matter what the class size.
>
> To use small-group discussions, the instructor divides the class into groups of three to five students. Each group is given a question or problem and asked to prepare a group response within a specified time. While students discuss the task, the instructor moves from group to group, monitoring students' progress, offering help when they need it, and noting areas of confusion for later review. When time is up, the instructor reconvenes the class and asks the groups (or a sample of them) to report their answers or conclusions. Depending on the nature of the task, group reports may stand as given, call for feedback or comment from the instructor, or stimulate further exploration and discussion (pp. 107–8).

In the textbook, the authors continued by listing activities that teachers in individual disciplines might use as tasks for small groups in their classes. For English classes,

> In order to explore how authors use different techniques for revealing and developing character, each of your groups will work on one of the following questions about Virginia Woolf's *Mrs. Dalloway.* 1. What impressions or insights do you have about Mrs. Dalloway based on what she reveals to the reader about herself? Support your comments by identifying passages in which she expresses her thoughts and feelings directly to the reader. 2. What impressions or insights do you have about Mrs. Dalloway based on the way you see her in interactions with other characters? Find excerpts in which her interactions with other characters provide insights into her character. . . . (pp. 108–109)

I didn't choose this example to make the textbook into a straw man I could knock down. Obviously, there are problems with the oversimplification involved in these textbook instructions. But not only is the attempt real, it also reflects what many teachers and students think about group work and its dynamic. First, they think of group work primarily as a kind of time-out or recess from the more typical work of the class in whole-room discussion. Second, they assume that all group endeavors are teacher directed and teacher monitored and that their limits are precisely defined in terms of the activity to be accomplished and the time allotted to completing it. The activity suggested with Virginia Woolf's (1953) novel follows these beliefs: the questions are carefully controlled, are similar to one another, allow for clear evaluation and response, and limit or eliminate students' own discussion about the novel if that discussion deviates from the focus the questions (and the teacher who has asked them) have set.

In *A Community of Writers,* Peter Elbow and Pat Belanoff (1995) attempted to make group activity organically a part of this textbook for first-year writers and encountered some of the same problems. Following are the questions they tell a writer to ask of a group during discussion of a draft of a paper:

> Which parts do you see most? Tell me in your own words what you see.
> Where do you feel the most energy, voice, and life in my writing?
> Which parts are the most believable?
> Are there places where you feel me trying to take the image where it doesn't want to go?
> What does the story mean to you? (p. 46)

Perhaps the biggest problem in attempting to give this kind of direction for group work is that it somehow kills the activity by defining and describing it so closely. Elbow and Belanoff's suggestions are not bad for writers to use, but they strike the ear as false. No writer would really ask these questions of his or her group in just that way, and the questions wouldn't proceed so neatly even if they were asked. Textbooks in general have trouble with groups because groups don't seem susceptible to the kind of pinning down that textbooks thrive on. Textbooks institutionalize practice, and the group—when it's working—almost always resists institutionalization.

The Problem of Training

If textbooks don't help teachers with group work, neither does most teachers' past experience. Few teachers have had any training in making group work productive (among college teachers, few have had any training in teaching) and little firsthand positive experience with groups. Experienced teachers have few good memories of school group work and little guidance in their preparation courses, much less in their content-area majors. Many of the comments that begin this chapter were from students who will be teachers or who are now teachers.

The physical place for a teacher in a classroom where groups are operating is a kind of metaphor for the problem teachers face with groups. Watch a teacher attempting group work for the first time in a semester, or with a classroom he or she is uncomfortable with. The teacher seems caught in a kind of no-person's land in the room, neither at the front of the room with his or her desk nor in front of the desk with a group. The teacher hovers, stepping back and forth, unwilling to join a group and risk losing all the others, unable to stand at the front of the room and be ignored. This discomfort with location makes many teachers avoid groups altogether, place them carefully at times during the class session when they have work of their own to attend to, or give direct, step-by-step instructions that allow them to make sure each group is doing its assigned tasks.

Unfortunately, there are many other cautionary stories of failed groups in a classroom. Those I've told here are meant to be suggestive— giving voice to what underlies much of the lack of success with the use of groups—for the students who see themselves as hard workers, for those who coast, and for the teachers who try to make both kinds of students work together in their small circles. Underlying all these problems with groups is a mistrust, sometimes a fear, of what might take place in a group where Authority, as it's defined in the teacher's role, is absent. This fear and mistrust guide both teachers' and students' reactions to groups and prevent them both from finding strategies for making their work with small groups rich and meaningful.

The Fear of Loss of Voice and Control in Groups

If you picture once again the teacher hovering between his or her desk and a small group, pacing, straining to listen and not to comment, bending, straightening, backing off, you can almost feel the teacher's discomfort. Why the dis-ease with this kind of classroom dynamic? Primarily, I think it's because teachers—and their students—have been socialized in school to believe that one voice matters more than all the rest: the teacher's voice. If his or her voice is missing or addressed to only a portion of the class, something seems wrong. If a teacher is not at his or her desk or the board or the overhead, the teacher's out of place.

Years ago when I began teaching, I attempted to use groups often in my class of ninth and tenth graders. I understood little then about learning theory or development, and I hadn't read much composition or reading research that would have given me strong support for my efforts. I just liked the idea of my students' having more of a literal say in the way our class hour went, and so we worked in small groups often. I understood even less about administrative agendas or institutional philosophy. So I was stunned one day when the principal of my school, seeing my groups at work, called out to me in a loud stage whisper, "I'll come back and observe some day when you're teaching!" Other teachers have told me a similar reaction from their colleagues or supervisors has prevented them from continuing to experiment with making groups work or has made them feel guilty about their activity in small groups.

I continued to use groups, and it's been long ago enough now that I've forgotten whether or not I felt guilty or worried that my principal would object. But I know that groups were a kind of violation of what my principal might have thought of as the natural order of things, and for this reason they remained if not frightening, a little suspect to him. Mr. Ramsay was uncomfortable with sitting and observing something he didn't know how to look at, I think. He couldn't comment on my lecture or large-class discussion or the way I introduced an assignment to the class. And so, to him, there was nothing to observe about my teaching. He couldn't hear my voice above those of the students.

* * *

A photograph in my local newspaper (Figure 3–4), documenting the first day of school in the fall, tellingly reveals the dominant perception that the teacher's voice is central. In such a scene, it's not surprising that teachers and students feel less than comfortable when that most important voice is silent or muted. Students at the beginning of a semester will break up into groups and spend the first few minutes of

Figure 3–4   The central role of the teacher's voice

their time looking around the room for the teacher, or waiting for the teacher, or getting up to go ask the teacher a question. The male student mentioned in Chapter 2 who left his group in the middle of group planning so that he could talk to the teacher signaled not only his lack of trust in the group's authority, but also his belief in the authority of the person who was really in control.

*   *   *

Shirley Brice Heath reported in a talk at the 1998 National Council of Teachers of English (NCTE) Spring Conference that despite all the highly visible commentary about interactive learning or collaboration, less than two percent of a class period is devoted to anything but teacher talk. In *Failing at Fairness,* David and Myra Sadker (1994) wrote about the perceived need for control and order in the classroom that so often prevents talk, especially talk from girls, both white and of color:

> The classroom is the only place in society where so many different, young, and restless individuals are crowded into close quarters for an extended period of time day after day. Teachers sense the undertow of raw energy and restlessness that threatens to engulf the classroom. To preserve order, most teachers use established classroom conventions such as raising your hand if you want to talk (p. 43).

Teachers, then, limit talk because they fear the loss of control that will likely ensue once talk begins. And a loss of control is exactly what teachers want least in their classrooms. They are, after all and even with their state-approved authority, only one voice among twenty-five or thirty, and they might never recover the floor if it's completely taken away by others—especially others who may not be completely socialized to the rules of behavior in school and in institutions. The photograph in Figure 3–4 was taken in a first-grade class on the first day of school. Socializing to authority figures begins early.

When large-class discussion does become more free and interactive in a class, and the talk or the questions get lively, students may begin to "get out of control," and lose the decorum of hand raising and waiting. When this happens, the Sadkers' research shows, boys begin to dominate:

> Our research shows that boys call out eight times more often than girls. . . . Whether male comments are insightful or irrelevant, teachers respond to them. However, when girls call out, there is a fascinating occurrence: suddenly the teacher remembers the rule about raising your hand before you talk. And then the girl, who is usually not as assertive as the male students, is deftly and swiftly put back in her place (p. 43).

Large-class discussion, then, especially when it's designed to provoke stimulating interaction from students, often limits and constrains women and privileges men. This kind of discussion, however, doesn't violate classroom order as groups do, and thus it's seen as more comfortable, even more natural, than that in small groups. The orderly, or even slightly disorderly, large-class discussion still has at its core the teacher's authoritative presence and voice. Many students in my Teaching of Writing class, the class that helps prepare them to student teach, remember with fondness, even with hero worship, Robin Williams' portrayal of John Keating, the iconoclastic teacher in *Dead Poets Society* (1988). Mr. Keating invites—demands—participation from his class of twenty or so white, upper-class New England boys. But he never loses his own voice as he directs the class to tear pages from their textbook, recite on stage, and stand on desks. If the boys in a small group had all stood on desks at their own discretion, they might have been viewed as budding hoodlums or revolutionaries, not males Keating was directing to be freethinkers.

Test yourself in your classroom and you'll hear how much your own voice dominates and how little—despite your best efforts—your students have a voice in the conversation. In fact, one of the most important strengths of small-group work, and one I talk about in detail in Chapter 4, lies in its ability to make a chorus heard in a classroom that is usually so relentlessly a solo performance. However, the chorus is precisely the problem. Teachers and students fear what will happen when the many rather than the one have a say, when there is no single voice to dominate or direct, when there are many directions and many paths and therefore potentially many outcomes to any activity. The fear is simply the fear of chaos.

And institutions fear chaos in great measure because chaos produces, or can produce, change. It's a commonplace that institutions are slow to change, slow to respond to the need for alteration of rules, not to mention the structures that lie beneath these rules. In public schools, where "new" methods are touted, implemented, and abandoned with what seems to some parents and teachers bewildering speed, the problem often is that real change hasn't occurred and so the new methods or innovations have no chance of working. Teachers aren't given time or help in working with new theories or methods, so they have little invested in making these methods work. "I've tried that group work," one teacher told one of the student teachers I supervised last year. "That was years ago."

If structures don't alter to accommodate new ideas, the ideas will seldom succeed. An idea that teachers should teach in collaborative units will not work in a system that won't allow coteachers to take their planning periods at the same time. An idea that students work together on long-range projects won't work within a structure that makes teachers grade by evaluating one student's performance against that of the others. Change is difficult for institutions like schools and universities because there is such a need to know what counts as good, or real—what can be valued—and what can thus be evaluated in students' and colleagues' work. The teacher, in his or her function as the representative of the institution, decides what is good and valuable in the work of his or her students as they attempt to master the segment of the discipline being taught. Students don't make decisions about value or reality in these disciplines. If students have too big a voice, or if this voice is too loud, as is always the threat when small groups meet, students may come up with something that the teacher, or the institution, hasn't decided should count as worthwhile. The teacher worries that his or her expertise might be pushed aside if too many other voices—and many without expertise—counter it.

Normal Discourse and Its Alternative

The school uses and values what Richard Rorty (1979) in *Philosophy and the Mirror of Nature* called *normal discourse*, the language and conversation that occurs within a community of *knowledgeable peers*, defined by Rorty as a group whose ideas and work are guided by the same codes of values and assumptions. In normal discourse, as Rorty said, everybody agrees on the guidelines of discourse: the same "set of conventions about what counts as a relevant contribution, what counts as a question, what counts as having a good argument for that answer or a good criticism of it." The result of normal discourse is that participants agree about the truth and rationality of the statements (p. 320).

Teaching normal discourse is central to the work of the classroom at all levels; students are rewarded—as are teachers—for their ability to produce work in the normal discourse of the fields they are working in. The form of the quadratic equation, the materials and methods of the lab report, and the word-level analysis of the poetry explication, all these are elements of the normal discourse teachers want students to produce. And normal discourse encompasses elements other than form—voice, vocabulary, types of evidence, and style. As Kenneth Bruffee (1984) said, "Mastery of a knowledge community's normal discourse is the basic qualification for acceptance into that community" (p. 643).

This description of normal discourse and its function in the educational institution raises a host of issues, especially when it's applied to the uses of groups in the classroom. Some students, those already socialized to a school-speech normal discourse—that is, many middle-class and white students—might have a decided advantage in practicing and mastering the normal discourse of academic speech. The apprenticeship model that Rorty's and Bruffee's descriptions rely upon is also perhaps better suited for, and traditionally meant for, males in the culture who would take the reins of power as they acquired the tools of discourse they needed. Women, traditionally excluded from positions of power and influence, have often used discourse not regarded as normal in their speech. The recent recovery of women's texts—in the form of diaries, letters, journals, parodies, travel documents, and romance stories—shows how "abnormal" their discourse often was in terms of the "community of knowledgeable (male) peers."

The same is true for writers of color. African Americans, both women and men, have historically participated only marginally in the normal discourse of the culture, in part because they were denied participation in educational institutions that would have them practice this discourse. Dialect speech of many African Americans, including forms, tropes, uses of evidence, and voice and style, separated their discourse from the "normal discourse" of the academic environments they entered, once they were allowed to enter them, and, as many researchers have documented, caused significant problems for users of dialect speech in school.[1]

It might seem as though small groups would be ideal for practicing the skills of normal discourse in a small community, which would provide a context for exercising the discourse of the established community of "knowledgeable peers," and for thus moving toward acceptance in that community. But, as Bruffee (1984) pointed out, there is the problem of how students who are not yet members of that community of peers can help one another to enter it. And if women and minorities are part of the small groups, how might their discourse—which is perhaps even farther away than that of middle-class white males from the discourse of the community—affect the work of the group in trying to become part of the knowledgeable community? Bruffee's answer to the first question (he doesn't address the second) is that students all bring something with them to the circle; no student is "wholly ignorant and inexperienced" (p. 630). In addition, the teacher's structuring the work of the small group leads to use of normal discourse; his or her advice and monitoring aid students in becoming adept at the use of the normal discourse—its unspoken agendas as well as its explicit forms—in their own discourse. Bruffee concluded that students' conversations are important for themselves: the talk itself transforms their abilities to become part of the communities they're in school to enter. "They converse in order to reach consensus in answer to questions the teacher has raised about the text. They converse about and as a part of understanding. In short, they learn, by practicing it in this orderly way, the normal discourse of the academic community," he said (p. 645).

Bruffee's ideas about the role of groups in the classroom suggest that women and minorities can have just as much a voice and a part of

1. Henry Louis Gates, Jr.'s (1988) work on African American dialect speech in *The Signifying Monkey* established the complexity and range of African American dialects and their differences from what could be called *school dialect*. For further study of how dialect difference interferes with success in school, see especially the following: Ellen Cushman, Eugene Kintgen, Barry Kroll, and Mike Rose's *Literacy: A Critical Sourcebook* (2001; Elizabeth McHenry and Shirley Brice Heath's chapter "The Literate and the Literary"); Shirley Brice Heath's *Ways with Words* (1983); Eugene Kintgen, Barry Kroll, and Mike Rose's *Perspectives on Literacy* (1988; John Ogbu's chapter "Literacy and Schooling in Subordinate Cultures: The Case of Black Americans"); William Labov's *The Logic of Nonstandard English* (1970); and Geneva Smitherman's *Talkin' and Testifyin'* (1977).

the work in learning and building on normal discourse as other more privileged groups have. But the inequities of our stratified society, inequities made even more insusceptible to change because the culture so often refuses to acknowledge them, get played out in classrooms and in groups as well as in the culture at large. Biases and prejudices about class background, ethnic characterisitics, sex and gender roles, and race relations inevitably and unconsciously frame the conversation in the small group. And this means that women and minorities might not have any better chance at involvement and power than they have had traditionally in the world outside the classroom.

Yet teachers believe in the democratic ideal that suggests that everyone should have a voice and a forum in which to speak it. The group, in the way it speaks, retracts, revises, envisions, and recreates, models the way knowledge is generated and developed. Group work and the collaborative learning that ensues from it suggest that knowledge is made, not merely acquired; not simply discovered, but *made*. This model flies in the face of the institutional structure that places all authority in the hands of a textbook, an end-of-course test, or a teacher. In other words, group work values and nurtures something more than the "normal discourse" of the academic environment, and so has the hope of valuing the contributions of those who have not had access to this discourse or who have resisted it. Groups can help students learn to use the normal discourse of their fields of study but can also generate new knowledge that might move beyond what's accepted as normal.

Bruffee (1984) suggested that the kind of group discussion that generates new knowledge cannot be normal discourse since normal discourse maintains existing knowledge. Rorty's (1979) definition of *abnormal* is "what happens when someone joins in the discourse who is ignorant of conventions" or normal discourse, or "who sets them aside" (pp. 320, 339). According to Bruffee (1984), abnormal discourse in groups can "sniff out stale, unproductive knowledge and challenges its authority, that is, the authority of the community which that knowledge constitutes" (p. 648). Abnormal discourse would seem to be necessary to the kind of knowledge as generative model that many classrooms seek to nurture, but, Bruffee argued, abnormal discourse cannot be taught. Instead, students should be taught "practical rhetoric and critical analysis" in such a way that "students can turn to abnormal discourse in order to undermine their own and other people's reliance on canonical conventions and vocabulary of normal discourse" (p. 648).

Bruffee continued, "Challenging the traditional authority of knowledge in this way, collaborative learning naturally challenges the traditional basis of the authority of those who teach" (p. 649). In saying this, Bruffee named the central paradox teachers face in using and nurturing groups in their classrooms. Teachers gain authority from being the designated representatives of normal discourse, the *informed readers* [to use Stanley Fish's (1980) phrase] in the group who, by virtue of their preparation and their experience, can speak for the community of knowledgeable peers and invite their students into this community. But, they are also agents of change, and must be if new knowledge is to be generated, if students are to think critically, and if new voices are to be heard. The conflict between being gatekeepers and gate-crashers looms large for teachers, and it gets played out in the way teachers make assignments, evaluate prose, assign grades, and decide on texts. Their solution to the conflict they face is often to downplay the "abnormal voices" they hear in students' texts, and in students' groups, but the conflict remains, especially for the many teachers who so deeply desire more interaction and interest among their students.

A Place for the Abnormal

It's easy to see how groups work to foster abnormal discourse, and this should be one reason, although a slightly disconcerting one, for valuing them. But how teachers reconcile their desire and need to teach the tools of the trade, the normal discourses of their fields, and their equally strong need to allow students to teach them, and their fields, new ways of thinking is a more difficult matter. In her landmark work on BEV (Black English Vernacular) and education, *Talkin' and Testifyin'*, Geneva Smitherman (1977) wrote of how misconceptions about language and correctness often dominate the discourse in a classroom and kill interactive discourse among students and between students and teachers. Smitherman's book is about abnormal discourse, or at least abnormal discourse in the educational institution. "Despite the American ideal of equal opportunity for all, the oppressive 'doctrine of correctness' still abounds," she said. "It is kept alive not only by popular misconceptions about 'standard' English and 'correct' speech, but also by persistent myths about languages in general" (p. 191). This myth correlates with another about some languages' being "primitive" or "underdeveloped" and still another that there is just one "true" language in any culture and that all the rest are inferior dialects. For abnormal discourse to have a chance in the classroom, these myths—disproved by linguists over a century ago—have to be abandoned in educational practice.

Smitherman began such work with her book, in which she moved from the "normal" academic discourse that you hear in her preceding statement to this kind of speech:

> For example, the call-response dynamic is integral to the communica-
> tion system of Black English (as y'all now know, right?). Since black
> communication works in this interactive way, then maybe it means
> that black students who are passively listening aren't really learn-
> ing. Teachers can capitalize on this dynamic by recognizing that they

should expect—indeed, be desirous of—some "noisy" behavior from black kids. It means they diggin' on what you sayin' (p. 220).

Smitherman's rhetorical point in sliding from academic speech to dialect speech reinforces her argument about correctness and communication, about the social and cultural uses to which linguistic variation can be put.

Some educators have written movingly of how their perspectives changed in education as they worked with small groups whose abnormal discourse allowed both the group and the teacher to come to new understandings. Their experiences help teachers envision how the conflict between preserving or transmitting knowledge and making way for new knowledge can be mitigated in the work of small groups. Mike Rose's small group of learners who talked together about poetry, mentioned in Chapter 1, insisted that the poems they liked be included in the discussion. Only then could they begin to line up their poems with the canonically approved poems Rose was teaching them. Rose not only had to allow the group's abnormal discourse—its fondness for sentimental, obvious poetry—to find a place in the classroom, but also had to adjust some of what he felt "counted" as poetry, what "counted" as a good response. The woman who wrote a poem "like Mike likes" at the end of the narrative let Mike into the circle she and her fellow Learning Line members had been establishing, not the other way around. This small truth about control and change that affects both teacher and student shows the potentially transformative way that small groups can work in the classroom.

Paulo Freire provided a similar instance of how the small group alters a teacher's agenda and challenges a teacher's authority. In *A Pedagogy of Hope,* Freire's 1994 account of his lifelong tranformative process as a teacher and a writer, he spoke of a workshop he gave years before in Brazil. In the workshop, he explained his ideas about education and authority and used Piaget and learning theory to explain these ideas to his group of learners. After his presentation, a man in the group stood and gave a talk, which, Freire said "seared my soul for good and all." The man began by thanking Freire for his fine words. But he "and my fellow workers" had questions: "Dr. Paulo, sir—do you know where people live? Have you ever been in any of our houses, sir?" In describing his conditions and those of his group, he compared his life with Freire's:

> It's one thing to come home, even tired, and find the kids all bathed, dressed up, clean, well fed, not hungry—and another thing to come home and find your kids dirty, hungry, crying and making noise. And people have to get up at four in the morning the next day and start all over again—hurting, sad, hopeless (pp. 25–26).

The man pointed to Freire's lack of understanding about the material conditions of his life and thus challenged Freire's authority to make meaning for him and for the group of workers in the audience.

Freire recalled complaining to his wife later that evening that the group didn't understand him. "Could it have been you, Paulo, who didn't understand them?" she said. "I think they got the main point of your talk. The worker made that clear in what he said. They understood you, but they needed to have you understand them. That's the question" (pp. 26–27). This experience led Freire to begin the process of learning that the educator must change to "be up to an understanding of the world the people have" (p. 27). The group of workers in Recife altered Freire's thinking and his action, becoming the basis for an education program, built upon the stories and lives of people, the words and ideas meaningful to them as the foundation for their own literacy. Freire's knowledge of the world shifted and expanded as the group asserted itself within the discourse he had presented in his talk.

As Geneva Smitherman (1977) said, "Certainly it is easier to work on fitting people into the mainstream than to change the *course* of the stream itself" (p. 241). But the experience of these two teachers shows that both things can and do happen: Students do get fit into some mainstream; their work with teachers and with one another inevitably allows them to transform their own ways of thinking and writing into ways that connect to others more explicitly and smoothly. But students working together also force changes in the flow of the mainstream, alter currents, add new riverbeds, and expose old ones, and teachers are in the unique position of helping both to happen.

How to Change the Course of the Stream: Finding Voice

The Circle in School: Small Groups in the Classroom

> I feel that the workshops are very helpful. When I was writing my storytelling paper, I tried to keep in mind what everyone said about my first paper. I was scared that everyone would not like my paper that they read, and maybe be harsh and pick out every little thing that I did wrong. But they didn't Thank God. This workshop made me feel more secure about my writing.

The preceding excerpt, written by a woman who recorded in her journal her fears about an early group session where each group member was reading drafts of one another's essays, voiced the writer's anxiety about group response. Her past experience had made her feel both unsure and untrusting about sharing her ideas with her fellow classmates and had made her believe that the group's role would be very much what she had no doubt learned to expect from her teachers: to "be harsh and pick out every little thing that I did wrong." This student showed she was beginning to develop a sense of her own writing and her ability to let others hear her writer's voice.

"Women who have spent years learning the lessons of silence in elementary, secondary, and college classrooms have trouble regaining their voices," the Sadkers (1994) reported in their research (p. 10). Women are often afraid, in fact, of their voices. After a role-playing exercise where college instructors played the parts of schoolchildren in a demonstration of how sexism works in classroom dynamics, the Sadkers asked one woman who was consistently not called on by the teacher, "Why didn't you just shout out an answer? The men were calling out." She responded, "It never occurred to me to do it." Then she said, "No . . . that's not true. I thought about it, but I didn't want to be out there where I might get laughed at or ridiculed" (pp. 11–12). This fear of ridicule was also clear in the preceding response.

David Sadker conducted the role-playing exercise repeatedly in workshops across the United States, demonstrating sex bias by teachers who blatantly and offensively ignore female students. "Almost always," the Sadkers wrote, "the adult women, put back into the role of twelve-year-olds, sit and say nothing; once again they become the nice girls watching the boys in action" (p. 12).

The fear of voice expressed by women and girls in the Sadkers' survey and in the comment from my student indicate how much work teachers need to do to encourage the voices of their students. And, as my student's comment suggests, the small group can be a way for female students to begin to let themselves hear their own oral and written voices.

The Circle Out of School: Groups in the Community

Groups working outside the educational institution have had a long history of giving voice to people who are otherwise disenfranchised or whose ideas might not find a forum in the wider culture. These groups often operate as a comment on and an answer to injustice or wrong-headedness among traditional institutions that have denied the group a place or a voice in these institutions. For example, Anne Gere's (1997) study of women's groups in the United States provides a record of how this commentary and support operated for the diverse groups of women who joined women's organizations in this country during the early part of the twentieth century. Speaking of African American women's clubs, she wrote that African American women embraced their racial identity by naming their national federation the National Association of Colored

Women and countered the racist descriptions of them in white culture by addressing one another with titles of respect, Miss or Mrs., in club records. Mormon clubwomen identified one another by religious designations in contradistinction to the denigration of their religion by the larger culture; other women used their own names rather than their husbands' as an assertion of their own identity. As Gere said, "By naming themselves and recording the conversations that recorded these names, clubwomen wrote themselves into the larger society on their own terms, appropriating and redefining such words as *club* and *women* to describe themselves and their activities" (pp. 7–8).

The women's voices in the club papers from the many women's organizations Gere surveyed in her book—Jewish women's federations, working-class women's clubs, African American women's-organizations, and middle-class white women's clubs—are strong and positive. All these groups provide a way to hear women who were largely silent in a society that gave them little power or freedom. Through their literary circles and reading groups, an integral part of many women's clubs, these clubs gave nontraditional and noncanonical writers an audience and a chance. African American women's reading groups, for example, offered a nonwhite perspective on racism and exploitation, the Civil War, and Reconstruction, in their reading of writers like Frances Harper, Phillis Wheatley, W. E. B. DuBois, Anna Cooper, and Ida B. Wells. As all these groups read with other women, they developed their own *interpretive community* of readers, to use Stanley Fish's term. And in this community they could examine their own experience and opportunities for change. They could determine as well their own values for what they read, something that became increasingly galling to the newly emerging profession of English studies at the turn of the century.[2]

Groups outside school have a better chance of making this kind of comment since they are not bound by the structures that keep the small group and the large institution in their respective places. Gere's earlier (1987) study of writing groups, *Writing Groups: History, Theory and Implications,* made a similar point to the one she implied in her 1997 *Intimate Practices*: groups work better outside educational settings because they are self-directed and create their own styles of discourse. "Self sponsored writing groups," she said, "incorporate this cluster of caring connection, non-rule bound, nonhierarchical characteristics" (p. 51). Groups within school typically place emphasis on rules rather than relationships, she pointed out. And grades get in

2. Gere (1997) noted that English departments and professional literary organizations denigrated women's reading experiences in their club reading groups, calling them dismissively "amateurs" and "housewives" and suggesting that only professionals knew how to value and interpret literary work (see pages 130 ff.).

the way. Questions like "What did she say we were supposed to do?" so common in the students' responses that began this chapter, don't appear in the minutes of women's groups or club notes.

One reason that teachers want to use groups in the classroom is to begin to hear the voices that are often silenced by the professional stance of teachers and texts. For this to happen within the educational setting, students have to be allowed to determine some of their own agendas, as Gere's study implied, and they have to be willing to face the conflict of opinion and value that emerges when people are allowed to use their own ways of knowing to respond to issues and to texts in the circle of the group. "Writing groups have existed for more than two hundred years, but the continuing 'discovery' of them demonstrates the extent to which they have remained on the edge of educational consciousness," Gere noted (p. 52). For groups to work toward the end of better learning and of racial and gender equity, groups have to become deeply a part of the educational mission, rather than a curricular add-on or "new" trick. Once they have been invested with some of the same goals that groups outside education have claimed—to give power to those without it, to provide support for mutual agendas and interests, to foster change and growth among members—they will begin to offer solutions to some of the most serious educational problems facing schools and universities today.

How to Change the Course of the Stream: Making Groups Work

Facing Conflict

One of the most difficult issues facing students and teachers who wish to use groups in the organic way this book has been arguing for is the conflict that may ensue within a group when group members are voicing opinions and ideas. Thomas Fox (1994) described one such conflict in his article on the problems with race and gender in collaborative classrooms. He randomly set up groups of three at the semester's beginning, and after class, one male student approached him to ask for a change. When Fox questioned the student, he responded, "They're both black girls. I don't think I could help them. I've never been around black people. I don't know anything about them." Fox asked him to stay in the group, and the student accomplished his work, but, as Fox said ruefully, "I never sensed that he wished to learn anything from his group members" (p. 111).

The substance of Fox's writing class was based on the theme of race and gender and how these attributes affect writing. He was particularly disappointed that this group didn't work given the theme, where "this process seemed ideally suited," and where for the white male student "this process would be most transformative." Instead, the group managed only perfunctory compliance to the tasks. "I had to give up the notion," Fox admitted, "that collaborative learning is automatically a democratic and transformative process" (p. 111).

Part of Fox's problem in his classroom and with his group was with the assumptions he held about how students work together. Fox seemed to assume that students understood the dynamics of good group work when they began it: the give and take, assimilation and accommodation, and listening and turn taking that good conversation requires. His disappointment in the young man who came to him with a bewildered "I don't think I can help them" is evident. Fox implied that the male student's lack of understanding of how to "help" was both sexist and racist. And it is clear that the student saw himself as the potential leader. There isn't a statement from him about how the African American female students could help him. But it's likely that this student simply didn't understand how negotiation in a group might work, especially when the work was to be centered on looking at one another's ideas and considering them. Had the young man ever been taught how his own opinions become strengthened or altered once he hears a diverging opinion from a peer? Had he been encouraged to listen to another's voice, especially one so unlike his own?

Another part of Fox's problem was the mistaken belief that talking about the very issues that the group embodies, sex roles and race relations, will make it automatically easy for the group to share and interact. Race and gender are fine topics for classrooms to discuss and use as issues to explore in writing. But to assume that they become less-loaded topics because both sexes and black and white are represented in the group is not warranted. In fact, these issues sometimes become even more difficult to discuss when the makeup of the group makes the issues visible and personal.

Most crucially, Fox, like many of us, wanted to believe that simply placing students together—different races, different classes, different sexes—will mean that understanding will occur, that *transformation* will occur, primarily the transformation of the more powerful group member—the white, the male, the upper-middle-class, the European, the higher-SAT-scoring student. As Fox's story shows, this assumption doesn't always, maybe even doesn't usually, prove accurate. And teachers like Fox are left disappointed in students and in the group process.

If the small group offers possibilities to hear more voices and mutes the voice of the teacher, it doesn't necessarily live up to these possibilities any better than the large open-discussion sessions that the Sadkers observed in their research study. I learned this truth through hard experience; like the teachers who moved students' desks around and called it group work, I gave students work to do in groups and assumed that everybody would get opportunities to talk and participate in activities. I especially believed that women, who are typically more able to speak out in small, informal situations like the small group, would benefit from my strategy of making the small group the most important classroom unit. Like Fox, I discovered I was wrong.

My lesson came in a class preparing students to student teach in elementary, middle grades, and high school classrooms. It's a course that helps soon-to-be teachers consider literacy in all its perspectives— how they might teach writing, reading, and thinking; how they might connect how they will teach to the content of what they will teach. It's a difficult course because it makes conscious attempts to implicate theory in practice, including my own practice in the course itself. All students worked in small groups that remained constant throughout the semester, as they do in all my classes, and they produced two presentations, organized ideas about texts they were reading or issues the class was discussing, set agendas for their own research, and responded to one another's writing. The group meetings required a lot of energy and cooperation as all good groups do when their work is something more than busywork and something deeper than peer group editing.

One group in the course comprised three undergraduate women and two master's degree students, one woman and one man. Each group member brought different interests and backgrounds to the group, who named themselves the Parrots: Sally and Tim were specializing in middle grades education; Heather was a drama major and actress who would complete student teaching in English and drama; Barbara was an elementary education major returning to school after years working as a hospital admissions clerk, a job she still held part time. Finally, Rhonda was a student completing her degree after having successfully finished student teaching eighth-grade language arts.

Rhonda first alerted me to the problems of this group. Like most teachers who use groups, I was engaged in monitoring all the groups' progress, listening in, asking questions, and talking to individuals occasionally. One group had a number of quiet, rather frightened students in it; one was composed of too many students who knew one another and left other members out by their use of an intimate conversational style. These problems are not unusual, and teachers who use groups often not only recognize them, but have learned how to act to change the dynamics subtly enough not to interfere with the group's operation. But I was surprised by the Parrots. First, the group comprised more "mature" students than those of any other group, more who were over the traditional age of undergraduate students. Second, when I passed the group, I always seemed to hear good talk and see people nodding. Their first presentation had not been very well managed, but I thought this was due to a lack of time for organizational planning. When Rhonda came to see me one afternoon, however, I learned that the Parrots were working poorly for reasons I had not suspected.

When Rhonda sat down in my office, it was clear she was out of patience. She mentioned her group's presentation by saying flatly that it "sucked." She knew why, she said. Tim was such a domineering force in the group that no one else had power to make group decisions or even, as she saw it, have any input. She described the group's last meeting. "Sally had a good idea about how to connect up our chapter presentation with a group activity, and we all started talking. Except Tim. He just sat with his head down, writing. Then, when we had paused, he looked up and said, 'Here's the way I planned it.' It had *nothing* to do with anything we wanted."

"Why did you go along?" I asked.

She sighed. "I guess we just didn't want to make waves, make it uncomfortable. And Sally is his friend. We felt bad."

Rhonda's reactions mirrored the descriptions of those of the women in the Sadkers' study. The women in the group didn't want to cause trouble or make anyone feel uncomfortable, so they buried their conflict. Rhonda, older than some of the others, and the only one to have finished her student teaching, was at least able to voice her concerns to me, if not in her group.

I began to watch the group, waiting to see how difficult the interaction between members was before confronting Tim. Following are my notes from a group meeting two days after Rhonda had come to my office:

> They sit in a circle that's too wide. It makes it hard for them to really hear one another. Rhonda is very far away from the others, and her expression is angry and distrustful. Tim is conscious that I'm sitting in; he keeps glancing at me. He asks a question: "Well, what do you think we ought to do?" Barbara laughs before she responds to him. But she does respond and he nods. And looks at me. I know he's saying, "I'm doing right now, aren't I? I'm giving them a chance."

Later, Tim came to my office to talk. He was upset at his midpoint evaluation because I'd given him a B and asked him to think harder about his journal and his group participation. He said about his group, "I'm trying to get them to do the kinds of things I know you want to see in our presentations and talks. They don't seem to want to do them." He seemed genuinely baffled, genuinely upset. I asked him if he'd thought about why they may seem unwilling, and he looked at me. "Maybe they don't like my ideas," he said finally.

The group got very little better during the semester. I talked to each member separately. Sally was unhappy and had tried to talk to Tim about why the group was so recalcitrant. "He doesn't understand that we might not like to be told how it could be done best. He doesn't un-derstand how since he's so motivated he should be the one to do it." She thought it might have something to do with his being a graduate stu-dent, although she was one herself. "What about Rhonda?" I asked. Sally replied, "Well, he might resent it a little that she's already done her student teaching and knows things about actual practice that he doesn't quite know yet." Sally was resistant when I mentioned gender. Rhonda had been too. They wanted to see this as a personality prob-lem, even when I brought up Tim's comment about his role as guide and theirs as followers. "I don't think he's a sexist if that's what you're saying," Sally said.

But this story is all about gender roles as they get played out in group interaction. The fact that this class made so much of group endeavor made group members conscious of how they were working together. But their attitudes about gender, especially their fear of labels and "essentializing" roles, made them shy away from any meaningful talk with one another about their difficulties. "It's easier just to let Tim de-cide," Heather said to me. "We manage to get some points across too." Despite my recommendations, the group never could talk to one an-other about their failures and frustrations. They talked to one or another woman and they talked to their teacher. No one, except Sally, and then very hesitatingly, ever talked to Tim or he to them.

Tim clearly saw his role as the leader in every group meeting. He thought he was doing what was best for the group and said so to me. The women in his group let him play leader because they knew he thought it was his role, even though it angered them and compromised the group's work.

Because these people all intended to become teachers, it was natural for me to ask them to write in their final portfolios statements about how their group work might influence their teaching. I was especially interested in Tim's comments: "I guess I need to learn how to value the comments of those who might not be as immediately forthcoming as some others. I've been taught this in my classes, how to draw out people, how to get them interested, and I didn't try this with my group very well."

As a teacher who believed in group work and in the way that groups can manage differences and difficulties if they're given space to do so, I was distressed by this group's experience. My reflecting on the group led me to rethink some assumptions I had made about how groups work toward more equitable spaces for women. Three small insights have helped me in the semesters since then to create in my classes better situations in which the men and women can interact responsibly in their small groups. In Chapter 5, I talk about some of the practices that have grown out of these perceptions. These ideas can help teachers move beyond the failures so often associated with groups and toward the transformative power the group offers to the classroom.

1. The virtues of groups—compromise, turn taking, and connection— all practices associated with feminism and with feminine attributes—can work against the group as well as for it. In this instance, the four women could not use these qualities to work toward more effective group interaction. In the name of compromise, they remained silent; in the name of cohesiveness and connection, they followed the rules laid out by one member. Tim operated from his own perspective, getting work done efficiently and quickly, persuading the group to his way of thinking. In his mind, group members were behaving well. Had there been someone else asserting a perspective, he might have made a place for that person's thinking in his own. But since the women offered little opposition or alternative, it was never strong enough to convince him to change his course of action.

2. Principles of equity must be established overtly in the group by its members and in classrooms by the teaching. Assuming that turn taking, for example, will lead to more female participation is not good enough. What I should have done as the teacher was to have made organizational plans that would help members account for their own work and for the effectiveness of their group. Group meetings with the teacher, reflections that discuss contributions and progress, and structures for changing responsibilities within groups all might have helped this one be more successful.

3. Neither gender is aware to what extent their reactions and habits are governed by role-playing and falling into cultural expectations for their gender. They are often resistant to being made conscious of these factors outside themselves, preferring to label reactions according only to individual personality. It's hard to make students aware of the way their behavior is affected by the roles they've been encouraged to play since birth, but it's necessary to help students understand the way that the individual perspective or personality is never merely that; that it's always connected to and affected by the social situation in which it's placed. That's a lesson for how people learn as well as for gender and race relations.

Although the Parrots were never successful because they were never collaborative in the way that they needed to become, all the group members recognized truths about their interactions that I hope have guided them in helping structure and nurture groups in their own classrooms. Tim's last comment in his journal reflects an understanding of just how hard it is to be a good group member: "To understand someone else's position is hard. Especially when you're sure you know the right way to go."

If students—maybe especially women—fear the conflict they might encounter in becoming honest and interactive in small groups, their teachers worry about potential conflicts nearly as much. Maybe one reason it took me so long to see the Parrots as dysfunctional was because I feared provoking even more conflict by acknowledging conflict was there already. Teachers can't help but worry about the differences of opinion that might emerge if students talk much together, or set the direction of the talk, which happens consistently when small groups function well. For a lot of reasons, including the need to get work done efficiently, teachers fear that students might digress from topics at hand or, worse, lose control—become emotional or boisterous or angry—if their talk isn't dictated by a clear agenda teachers predetermine.

John Trimbur (1989) has argued that teachers fear group work and the consensus that emerges from it as much as they fear conflict: "The fear of consensus often betrays a fear of peer group influence— a fear that students will keep their own records, work out collective norms, and take action" (p. 604). In large-class instruction, the teacher is in control, and students are "locked into a one-to-one relation to the teacher," who remains the repository of effective authority. Teachers fear what Trimbur has called *dissensus,* the speech of marginalized voices speaking in discourses of their own that comment on, resist, or rethink the consensual normal discourse they study—abnormal discourse, to use Rorty's term. In other words, they fear not so much the conflict that might ensue *within* a group as they do the conflict that might result between themselves and these groups.

Learning to write and speak in a community is more than learning to participate in the conversation and practices the community has ratified. To participate fully, learners must add their own voices to the discourse, must challenge the discourse they hear by making it connect to themselves. "The point of collaborative learning," Trimbur (1989) said, "is not simply to demystify the authority of knowledge by revealing its social character but to transform the productive apparatus, to change the social character of production" (p. 612). Students who work together in groups work toward connecting themselves to one another through language and asserting their own language within the group and in the larger context of the class and the community of learners. But they can't perform this work if teachers fear the conflict that dissensus presents—the speech of dialect, the odd form, the stream-of-consciousness comment.

In her 1994 book on teaching, *Teaching to Transgress,* bell hooks spoke of her anxiety with confronting diverse groups of students. She recognized that her "codes," her characteristic modes of approach and of writing, must shift to accommodate the various approaches among her ethnically, racially, and culturally diverse group of students and that this work is difficult for educators, who cling to old patterns out of fear of the change that the multicultural classroom presents:

> As I worked to create teaching strategies that would make a space for multicultural learning, I found it necessary to recognize what I have called in other writing on pedagogy "cultural codes." To teach effectively a diverse student body, I have to learn these codes. And so do students. This act alone transforms the classroom. The sharing of ideas and information does not always progress as quickly as it may in more homogeneous settings. Often, professors and students have to learn to accept different ways of knowing, new epistemologies, in the multicultural setting (p. 41).

hooks pointed to the give-and-take exchange that occurs between teacher and students and among students themselves in the classroom. Although she didn't indicate group work as the site of this exchange, her strategy embodies the essentials of group work, the simultaneous challenge and acceptance of ideas, the embracing of difference, the necessity of sharing and trust. hooks invited teachers to examine their practices in light of the multicultural classrooms we soon will all face, if we have not already, and to see this kind of negotiation of discourse as a method for making the classroom inviting and responsive to all the groups who will compose it.

Unmixing Motives

If teachers are to do as hooks and the experience of all the preceding teachers have suggested, they must renegotiate the space they make for groups in the classroom and the ways they evaluate the work that groups do. Many teachers have recognized how much the teaching of writing alters once they have made writing itself a subject for interactive discussion and response. In Marilyn Cooper and Michael Holzman's (1989) book, *Writing as Social Action,* Cooper noted teachers' changing awareness in her essay "The Ecology of Writing": "Many teachers in schools and colleges, as well as adult practitioners, have found that the Romantic paradigm of the isolated writer thinking individual thoughts simply does not work for writing instruction" (p. 7). The writer isn't isolated in a classroom and his or her thoughts aren't segregated from his or her friends' thoughts, and teachers have found that writing can improve once the truth of its social origins and consequences begin to be explored consciously.

But even though teachers recognize the falseness of the lonely-writer-in-a-beret motif that Cooper (mistakenly, I think) called *Romantic,* they have trouble acting on this perception in practice. When groups are often not understood as much more than a practical exigency to move students around the room, it's predetermined that they will never meet the goals of interaction and collaboration that they are meant to achieve. Kate's substitute teacher and my student teacher, who both placed desks in small circles and thus seemed to signal group involvement, failed to make groups' activities collaborative, so students never even looked at one another, much less worked together. They weren't deceived that they were "doing group work"; the teachers perhaps felt that students liked being in a different configuration, but they were clearly worried about what the students might do with groups once they moved into that configuration.

And, even more significantly, a professed belief in the connected group of writers acting in community gets consistently undermined by evaluation procedures in many schools and colleges. Group work ends up being more or less useless if the real, or final, purpose for group work is always individual achievement. The student at the beginning of the chapter who received an individual grade based on her group's performance (she had done excellent work; her colleagues had done "terrible" with the result that all group members received a C for their effort) was caught in a trap that classroom group work often falls prey to. A group simply cannot function well if the primary result is that individuals within the group are assessed on the basis of the work of others in the group. When teachers make group work the vehicle for this kind of evaluation, the motives for activity within the group become strained and mixed. Students then feel an understandable sense of betrayal if other group members don't achieve as much as they themselves have, feel frustrated if other group members are less adept or skillful at the tasks to be accomplished than they themselves are, and feel impatient with a group process that simply slows or diminishes work they could complete with greater speed and accuracy alone. Involvement, accommodation, and remaking in a group process are activities that conflict with being graded individually—or at least students perceive the conflict.

In Chapter 5, I talk about possible strategies to confront both these issues: how groups can be evaluated both fairly and effectively and how groups can be made an organic part of classroom instruction. But before teachers can put strategies in place, they must clearly assess their motives for using groups in a classroom in the first place. Most experienced teachers wouldn't move students into small circles to make it *look* as if they were making use of group work, as my inexperienced student teacher did in order to please me, but many experienced teachers do put group work into a lesson in more or less random ways without considering the rationale, the outcome for students, or the belief about learning that motivates the use of the group in the first place. Partially because they haven't been encouraged to investigate rationales and outcomes, teachers use groups but sparingly—if there's time in an overcrowded class period, if there's a dead space where students seem starved for talk with one another, or if the class is responsible enough to handle "the freedom," as one teacher said to me. Group work seen in these ways is a reward for students who have already proved they are socialized into the normal discourse of the classroom well enough not to go too far outside its bounds once they talk together.

Whose Group Is It Anyway?

Wayne, an English education student, soon to be teaching his first high school class, worried about the loss of control that autonomous groups in the classroom could elicit. He noted that most groups are not successful, and felt the teacher is to blame:

> First, teachers often do not provide good, concrete instructions to the groups, and as a result, the groups flounder and normally come up with an unfocused, less than satisfactory effort. Group directions need to be clear, precise, and preferably written as well as oral. Related to this issue is the need for the teacher to provide periodic checks with each group so that questions can be answered, feedback given, and course corrections made if necessary. The instructor needs to be available, but not intrusive.

Wayne saw the group dynamic as guided and monitored by the teacher's authority and believed that without the teacher, in fact, groups would "flounder." Students who move into their circles and begin to ask "What did she tell us?" "What are we supposed to do?" understand that the group belongs to the teacher, and that they have just been invited into the circle to fulfill the tasks the teacher has decided upon. So, is it the teacher's group or the students' group? Who decides what counts as good talk? Who makes decisions about who should talk? Who determines how the activities will build or what should be written or spoken to the larger group of the class?

I've begun to answer these questions in these first chapters. Why do we use groups? Because we know that things happen in them that don't happen with us at the front of the room. Mike Rose saw that; I've seen it. Over and over again. Students find their own way, learn to challenge and transform their own thinking, and take hold of their own ideas and the ideas presented to them in different, more productive ways when they are involved in an activity together—solving a problem or coming to terms with a new concept. Underlying teachers' desire to make groups work is a persistent belief in the value, the necessity, of practical action, of negotiation, of articulation, and of play. These are all the things that groups can do, all the things that Vygotsky and

Piaget and a host of other learning theorists have told us are crucial to learning. That's why we use them, why we *should* use them. And when we understand these underlying rationales, we begin the process of *method,* of making action out of belief.

Once teachers come to terms with the fact that groups belong to the students, teachers learn how to set guidelines and provoke interactions in genuine ways. And they give students the path toward making each member responsible for the way the group works and succeeds. Students, finally, must learn to deal with one another without the constant mediating presence of the teacher.

Working It Out

The circle breaks and opens. "I'm a little upset about my group," one student wrote to me. "I feel that the others are not at the point in their lives when they can take this class seriously and maturely. Not that it's supposed to be *serious* and *mature* all the time, but I get frustrated when the others in my group are doing work for other classes during our time together. Perhaps this will get better with time. I believe that I am contributing and feel comfortable in speaking within our community. Sometimes, I have to tell myself to keep my thoughts to myself because I like to speak my opinion."

All the group members in Catharine's circle were women, and I watched them, the day after I had read Catharine's journal, move together in a circle, although one stayed slightly on the perimeter and often appeared to be looking down rather than at her group members. Only one student in the group—Catharine—was white, and this fact complicated her feeling of frustration with the group. She didn't want to make a big issue of what she felt were problems with the group's willingness to work, in part because she worried a little—even though she knew her group members from other classes and they were friends— that it might become an issue of race. "I really don't want to be the good girl, the white girl tattletale," she told me. "That's not what's going on here. Everybody is smart and good at what they do. I just want to feel more like they are ready to do the work."

When Catharine and her group worked later in the week on revising ethnographic studies of learning situations for final portfolios, I asked them to write about what they had discussed. Following is the record of their collaboration, written by Catharine in her group's journal:

> *Jayne* (Central YMCA Nursery): Jayne feels like she needs more detailed information to write her ethnography. She wants to focus more on the specific sections/headings of her ethnography.

Artifacts brought: Bright blue octopus stuffed toy

Group response: Concentrate on details! Do the paper for yourself, not for Hepsie.

    Natalie (Evangel Fellowship Church of God worship service): Natalie feels the need to be more specific and pay attention to individuals that she finds interesting, rather than the group. She wants to include the way these individuals affect the group. She also wants to incorporate her culture's use of audio and video equipment.

Artifacts brought: History of the Church of God; Affirmation of Faith web page

Group response: Focus on how an individual affects group. *State* the obvious patterns.

    Catharine (Higher Ground Baptist Church worship service): I just need to get my thoughts organized and figure out what headings I will include. I want to focus on what makes this culture unique, and how it is not the stereotypical church service. I want to include the differences I find between the different types of people there, yet how they find one common bond.

Artifacts brought: Church bulletin, visitor card, hymnal

Group response: Make sure you include your take on and opinions about the patterns, not just the facts. And talk about who's the authority, who's the teacher.

    The group began to work through some of the issues that had troubled Catharine in her journal response. (One student, the least invested member of the group, was absent on the draft day, and this no doubt added to the feeling of real work accomplished as they thought about revision together without the presence of an uninterested bystander.) The record of what they wanted, what they brought, and what the group thought gave each group member encouragement to continue with a task—write an ethnography of a small culture they could observe as both insiders and outsiders and where learning was taking place—that they were unfamiliar with, and allowed them to think about what they still needed to work on for their finished pieces. There is satisfaction in the tone of this small outline of the group's work, and their mutual responsibility became even greater as they continued to work together during the rest of the semester.

The group's presentation. Late in the semester, each group in this Teaching of Writing class made presentations on one element that seemed to the group important to nurture in a writing class. Catharine's group chose imagination as their theme, and they worked well together to create an engaging presentation. After the presentation, I made comments to the group and to individuals within the group to evaluate their performance. In this case, I commented as follows:

> Dear Friends and Fellows [this group had altered their "bird" name to one more to their liking]:
>
> You all did a good job with translating the chapter into practical and sound advice for teaching the skills of literacy to any kind of class. You seemed to work well together too, as you moved from person to person. I particularly liked it when you interrupted one another every so often to add a comment or clarify a point. That's the mark of a group thinking together about a project rather than seeing their own little part as the only issue in the presentation. I would have liked you to *define* imagination at the beginning more carefully so that the class would see how far away it is from the kind of "creative writing" that mostly characterizes it. All of you did a good job with applying the main issues in the chapter to real activities.

Then I responded to each student individually. I said to Catharine:

> Excellent approach to your class. You look right at people, ask questions that you really want to know the answer to and read aloud well. I really like the way you made your readings connect through your discussion and application of the word *juxtaposition*. That ability to make all parts fit together organically is a primary tool for a teacher.

I made similar comments to Jayne and Natalie, praising them for making a presentation that showed their working together and sharing the responsibility. The uninvested student had, just about at this time, asked for a withdrawal from school because of personal problems. Her absence made a great difference in the group's motivation and activity. At the end of the semester, I asked the group to comment on its work, and Catharine said aloud to her group, "I've learned so much from you all about how to listen. I've really begun to figure out what it means to have everybody pulling together. Finally." They all laughed. Natalie said, "I learned a lot from Catharine and from Jayne too. Even from Sheila. We've got to be willing to share with each other, and not be afraid."

What could have been an unpleasant or a difficult experience for all these students turned out to be a positive one, in great measure because they worked out their issues together—in their talk, in their journals, and in writing. When I talked with them and then evaluated their presentation, they saw that their individual effort mattered both to the group process and to me. They recognized that their individual achievement was part of the group's performance. And they saw their group effort as something beyond their individual contribution.

The Friends and Fellows group learned how to negotiate their way through conflict with little reliance on me except as a sounding board in their journals. Negotiation is a key element that comes only when students realize that they, not the authority or teacher, are responsible for making the group work. In a graduate seminar a few semesters ago, one student (the only male and the only African American in his group) wrote about the presentation he and his group were planning:

> Understandably, some group members were less than enthusiastic about the prospect of not having a formal presentation; what if we don't cover all of the material? how do we keep control of the discussion? what about the five areas we are supposed to concentrate on? would that count as a presentation? and so on.
>
> Frankly I think the discussion strategy would be something Rose would approve of. It engages the student, it gives the discussion leader the chance to get around normal classroom barriers of communication (one-way communication, from teacher to student), it is adaptable to the situation. But I also understand the fear of walking into a classroom not knowing exactly how the period is going to take shape. So I was amenable to the ideas presented for making our group presentation more order-oriented. And I think our final decisions will make for both an interesting and an informative session.

Jaime negotiated his desire for a more open-ended discussion with other students whose need for order made them fear the looseness of the informal approach. He listened to the others and realized he could make adjustments and still have the presentation work.

How the Process of Working Together Evolves

Groups sometimes work out their problems and their strategies in ways that aren't even visible to the teacher in the classroom. Unless they comment in journals or loudly to one another, the process of assimilation and accommodation, of negotiating difference, and of learning tolerance and support are undercurrents to the task at hand. But as the group works, its circle expands, breaks, and reforms to listen to the voices within it. It must break and reform, so that women and minorities and others who've been silenced so long can find a place and a forum. A few years ago, I taught a class on social construction theory and collaboration, and I asked students to keep journals of their group work. Because these were graduate students reading much theory and teaching composition courses themselves for the most part, they wrote with energy and insight into the process. What follows is part of the journal of several students—all women—who illuminated much about the workings of a group that for teachers and outsiders often seems mysterious. These four women described in their journals how their collaboration in talking about the readings for the semester, sharing their writing, and producing a collaborative piece during the course of the semester proceeded:

> We did a lot of personal writing and reflection, then coming together to talk and formulate the paper as a whole, going away, bringing together, etc. . . .
>
> When we finally came to a day where we thought, "Today is the day when the paper will be completed," we had some problems. (Hence, the frantic phone call to you at home.) We had done so much talking and discussing and relating to everything else on our collective minds, that the project had taken on a life of its own. To write it down seemed almost ridiculous, in the face of all the tremendous, life-changing-earth-shattering conclusions we had come to in our discussions. When we tried to say it, it looked so small and silly there on the computer screen, and as the three of us read and re-read what we wrote, we began the evil task of editing, except we were all editing for different things, and all viewing the language used to describe concepts and ideas which we all seemed to agree upon, from different perspectives—perhaps, from different styles.
>
> We sat before the computer, actively engaged in the understanding of linguistic meaning, and taking apart every sentence as if the slightest misplacement of a word, or a term thrown out to the reader and left undefined, would cause the downfall of civilization as we knew it.
>
> So Lucy and I decided to go to the grocery store to get some seltzer water, our favorite drink besides coffee, and suddenly the world changed. We both had that look in our eyes like at any moment we could break out into hysterical, uncontrolled laughter, and I think the people at the store saw it, because they seemed to avoid us.

The writer of this reflection wittily described the process she and her group members followed as they prepared the final version of a paper they were writing together. You can see their trust and friendship, and the honest way she described the difficulties of actually writing with another person. The "time-out" at the grocery store led to inspiration. And when they returned with their seltzer water, they began to work through some of their difficulties.

The mutuality of their discourse, and their work together, resulted in their successful collaboration throughout the semester. The fact that they were all women, socialized to engage in this kind of mutual support and interchange, was no doubt a related factor—although it should be remembered that it's the behavior of mutual interchange, learning, and support that was significant in this case. These women were willing to let go, to let themselves become interested in one another as well as in their work.

As Nel Noddings (1992) described it, these women modeled the "ethic of care" by listening with attention to one another and by genuinely fostering an attitude of belief in one another's intelligence and worth that made their writing together—even though they all talked about how hard this writing was—something thrilling. When I read these journals, I remember all these women so well, and I feel the sense of participation and relationship that characterizes their comments.

* * *

We work well together, we just needed the proper place to demonstrate it to ourselves and then to go back to the computer to do the same. Writing collaboratively is like shopping, especially if you love the language like you love food. Specific choices are important, some words don't look so fresh, and others are so new they need a sign to tell you the nutritional content and various uses.

When we finally finished this project, I still felt a certain amount of disjointedness about the whole—I think I wanted to edit some more, but knew it would be bad for my health. I was becoming obsessed. I still don't really have a notion of whether it was a "good" paper or not, because I feel that we still attempted to take on too much, but I'm glad that we did. I love that paper, even if it still needs work, because it represents the resonance I feel this semester with Amy, Lucy and so many other persons.... It can be overwhelming, at times, but it still makes me feel like I'm a part of something so much larger than myself. It places me within a living dialogue.

Their work together helps answer the questions that form the basis of the next chapter: How can we teach men and women to work together toward these shared negotiations; how can we use this space defined by the breaking circle—like a breaking wave, just at the point of change and growth—to challenge racial and ethnic barriers and the lack of communication and equity that attends these barriers?

Chapter Four

Race and Gender
The Role of Groups for Confronting Difference

As bell hooks (1994) reminded us in *Teaching to Transgress,* teachers carry the myth of the democratic, equal space into the classroom, and they use this myth to guide decisions about activities and curriculum in a classroom. But to do so they have to ignore the very real differences in background, experience, ethnicity, and socioeconomic class that students come into the classroom with and the very real differences teachers bring into the classroom themselves. To the extent that students' lives don't match with a mythical classroom identity—primarily middle-class, male, and white—there's a disjunction in what teachers see in their classrooms and what their classrooms are. Only when we acknowledge difference and use it can the classroom become what it needs to be, a place of trust where both teachers and students can cross from the safe boundaries of unquestioned assumptions into the wilderness of new ideas and divergent experience and opinion.

The small group can be seen, and has been, as almost anti-institutional, for the way that it can redefine the boundaries of conversation, challenge authority, question received knowledge, and promote more than one perspective on ideas. This may be one reason that small groups frequently have difficulty flourishing in the public school classroom, where time constraints and traditional assumptions about behavior and correctness control the classroom environment teachers create. The small group may feel too potentially disruptive to the individual classroom: "I was afraid they'd get *out of control,*" one of my soon-to-be student teachers told me, explaining why she had abandoned her group work five minutes after she began it. And the group may feel even more potentially disruptive to the institution itself. The principal who saw my group work as "not teaching" (discussed in Chapter 3) clearly considered the small group as possibly inimical to the act of teaching.

One way that my institution signals its distrust of groups is its physical arrangement of classroom space. Tables and chairs are placed in long horizontal or vertical rows in every room in the building that houses the English department, as well as Romance Languages, History, and Classics. When new desks replaced some aging furniture a while ago, a department chair made signs to put on each classroom door: "Move the chairs and desks back to their original positions when you leave the classroom!" These rooms are so stuffed with tables that students can't move chairs around to make a group circle; my request for one room that would be a permanent group-work room has gone unheard. Lines are normal, the message seems to be; circles are not.

* * *

For this reason, and others mentioned in Chapter 3, groups have usually had their greatest successes outside the classroom, where institutional constraints lessen or disappear. It's also true that these outside places—places where the academic protocol or institutional rules don't exist—can provoke the most threatening discussions because group members feel more able to be honest or "real" in their reactions to one another. Conversations in these groups can become disruptive or threatening, as the codes that guide group behavior in school are challenged or ignored in more open settings. Yet the negotiation and change that can occur when group members feel free to talk and listen openly is valuable, even necessary, for groups to succeed in the classroom and out of it.

For Robert Brooke, Ruth Mirtz, and Rick Evans, teachers who in 1994 studied the small group interactions of their composition students, an understanding of how students view groups aids in making real conversations possible. Asking students to come up with metaphors to describe their small groups, these teachers saw patterns emerging. Some students felt that their group was "like being with friends" or "like a family." Others saw their group as more tentative—like "meeting someone new." Still other students compared their small group to objects valued for their usefulness: an electric shaver, a set of jumper cables, or an athletic team. Some saw the group as alienating or frightening, and their metaphors showed their anxiety: fitting in at a biker's bar or finding a new church. The metaphors suggest how difficult or easy it might be for students to interact with one another, become interdependent, share ideas, and change opinions. These teachers concluded their discussion of metaphor by noting that "these metaphors show us that the emotional experience surrounding small groups is rich and complex, and that much of the character of this experience stems from the ways students are able to match their group interaction to other experiences they've had in the past" (pp. 34–37).

As this group of teachers indicated, students come to group work with preconceived ideas about how group sharing works and predetermined personal conversational patterns that affect how open and honest they might be about sensitive topics or about the diversity they might encounter within their own group. Understanding how much a person brings of him- or herself to the group begins the process of learning how to work well in a group, and these teachers' assignment to their students to describe their small groups in a metaphor provides one example of how to make students conscious of this truth. As Deborah Tannen pointed out in 1990, "We find ourselves caught in miscommunication because the very methods—and the only methods—we have of communicating are not, as they seem, self-evident and 'logical.' Instead, they differ from person to person, especially in a society like ours where individuals come from such varied backgrounds" (pp. 12–13). The real talk and mutual learning that can occur in groups happens when individuals learn to feel both free to contribute and responsible for the freedom of others to contribute. This chapter examines some ways that classrooms can encourage this double aim of freedom and responsibility in group talk and why it's important to do so.

Group Conflicts: Fear and Faith

The women's group that Jill McLean Taylor, Carol Gilligan, and Amy Sullivan wrote about in their 1995 book *Between Voice and Silence* had to confront some serious divisions in their group when they worked together to consider how culture, ethnicity, and gender drive the educational paths of a diverse group of adolescent girls they studied over several years. The women in the group had much in common as researchers who were deeply interested in the relationship between gender and authority and in how adolescent girls learn to assert authority in their interactions with others. This group was diverse as well, with members from various social classes, of a variety of ethnicities, and with varying family backgrounds and situations. Meeting together for months to talk about the girls they observed and to learn from and about one another, these women sometimes ran into serious disagreement in their discussions. They learned to be open and truthful with one another, and their common goal led them to attempt to foster collaboration and connection, but they discovered that one subject in particular caused turmoil and misunderstanding and threatened to derail their team effort.

Just as in the culture at large, race was their most dangerous territory for conversation. Tensions among the group reached a climax at one point on a retreat, when the women came to what the authors called in their book a *relational impasse* as one woman was asked to clarify her remarks about race and backed away, "moving into silence." Disagreement began to swirl around the conversation in questions about who was speaking and not, who was listening, who should side with whom, who was hurt, and who was protected by the group. The authors concluded from the incident that the women's group played out many of the tensions young girls of all races and ethnicities face in their adolescence. The authors characterized the conversational patterns they observed when the women were faced with conflict as "exclusion, scapegoating, resistance, and a kind of self-abnegating capitulation that, according to the girls in our study, often forced them into isolation and false independence or into complicity with relationships they experienced as false" (p. 91).

As one group member later described, the underlying issue was trust: "Something happens and the issue of trust suddenly becomes like a cliff—one false step and the fall is irrevocable" (p. 93). The group had to work through the tensions and the fears uncovered in their talk in order to resolve to stay together, and they had to find a way to trust one another as they did their research and study. One group member left the group, but the others talked through their problems and fears and continued their work together.

No wonder teachers are frightened of what might happen when issues of class or ethnicity or gender or—especially—race emerge in small-group discussion. Taylor, Gilligan, and Sullivan's experience shows that the fear is justified. When people in a group begin to know one another and understand the process of making conversation and meaning together, they might talk about issues or express opinions that others find wrongheaded or even offensive. For groups to feel comfortable with the kind of discussion that might ensue once they know one another and are honest about their own opinions or experiences, groups have to find a way to nurture the kind of trust that Taylor, Gilligan, and Sullivan's women's group needed to survive.

The power of groups to provoke just these kinds of discussions becomes one reason that the classroom group is sometimes a threatening entity in a class devoted to reasoned thought and decorum and to following the rules, taking turns, being polite, and not getting emotional. The potential for small groups to disobey the rules, forget turn taking, become rude, and get excited or distressed is all too real a possibility for many teachers. To combat the chaotic potential of groups, teachers have often taken on the role of caretaker or sergeant at arms in the group, monitoring both the kind and the amount of talk that groups perform in the classroom. They give precise instructions, hand out questions that have clear answers, and set limits on the time that groups may spend on their work and the kind of work that groups may perform. When teachers direct classrooms where students are already prejudged by a tracked class as *low achieving* or *at risk* or whatever euphemism the school derives to designate the students it has low expectations for, the problems of control over the groups become even more dramatic. Not surprisingly, classrooms where students have been tagged with labels that indicate their potential for disruption or failure seldom meet in groups.

As the preceding chapters have stressed, it's deeply important for all students to learn to work in groups for the development of their own thinking and writing, since group work mirrors the negotiation that thinkers go through when they encounter texts and ideas. For groups to work, it's crucial for groups in the classroom to learn to trust one another; once they do, they can learn to be good readers of one another's texts, and they can confront issues that are difficult to discuss, issues that continue to affect the learning of all students. Students can do their greatest work in groups, as they articulate and rethink cultural assumptions about difference, about race and gender, and about class and privilege. Taylor, Gilligan, and Sullivan's women's group eventually resolved the serious conflicts they encountered about racial biases because they trusted the process as well as one another.

The group of researchers in that study had some advantages over classroom groups that helped them overcome difficulties, interact responsibly, and succeed in their work. Unlike many classroom groups, they were engaged in real inquiry together. The process of their collaboration derived from shared goals and mutually understood beliefs about their project and its importance. Classroom groups succeed best when they learn to do this kind of real work as well. For this to happen, teachers must do more than allow groups to make students more-active participants, although that's one fine reason for groups. The small-group setting can provide a way for students to set their own paths of inquiry and to remake goals and products as they work together. In other words, when groups work well, they link organically the *knower* and the *known*, the student and the subject. This means that the small group justifies its own activity and creates its own knowledge. The group of women in Taylor, Gilligan, and Sullivan's study created new knowledge about ethnicity and the psychological growth of adolescent girls in their work together because they created their own questions.

The process of making meaning together in a small group has far-reaching implications for teaching. As Nel Noddings' (1992) work has shown, when a classroom provides a caring, trusting environment, students learn both to articulate ideas and opinions and to listen to others' opinions and ideas. In such an atmosphere, they learn the process of making meaning in collaboration and connection, finding where they differ and where they connect, and negotiating with one another as they speak and, especially, as they listen. Too often, however, we confine and limit a group's work by our refusal to allow this process to occur consistently among the small groups in our classrooms. Real trust and real talk don't get fostered in our small classroom groups for all the reasons I've talked about. It's comfortable to assume that the serious problems that plague our culture—of class division, economic disadvantage, and continuing sexism and racism—aren't of much concern to students as they become more-engaged readers and writers in our classrooms.

But if students are silent about these issues in their talk together in the small group that teachers facilitate, they find other ways to make their voices heard. I once encountered a group's negotiation outside the classroom, discussed next, that made me think hard about the need for classroom groups to confront the sensitive issues of race, gender, and class, and in even a larger sense, the need for my groups to feel the freedom to express ideas and to modify them together.

Group Work on the Bathroom Wall

In a stall in the first-floor women's restroom in the building that houses the English department on my campus, I found a record of a group's work in which they confronted and rethought race. It was an entire conversation played out on the wall—a long, interactive, rambling talk among what may have been twenty or more women writing to one another about racial dilemmas. Their talk was both impassioned and serious, and reading their words, I learned something new about the power of the group to negotiate ideas. Following is some of their dialogue:

> "Fuck the KKK and they momas"
> "t h e I r (hello, spelling!)"
> "Merely a syntax variation of dialect. No spelling or usage errors.
> I can do without the profanity though."
> "Mommas, mamas, race is not an issue it's an excuse."
> "To abuse people."
> "Humankind."
> "Don't worry. The African American race is outpopulating
> Caucasians. By 2014 whites will be the minority."
> "So will blacks! The Mexican American population will within
> 15–20 years outnumber us all."

"And we'll all be starving! (Overpopulation is not an answer to anyone's problems—the earth needs fewer people to feed and house, not more.)"

"I can't believe so many people are making race an issue. We are *all* humans."

"Over 200 years of slavery and racial discrimination make it an issue!!"

"I haven't done shit to you."

"Get over it!"

"Just so you know, I am a white Christian female who loves and treats *everybody* equally."

"You need to realize the numerous privileges you have merely *because* you are white. You personally may not see yourself as racist, but the very *institutions* we all live under *are;* no one can escape that. Think of how there are more *black men* on death row than anyone else, or the fact that *black women* are being blamed for this country's economic crisis, when the majority of people on welfare are *white*. Also, welfare makes up less than one percent of the country's budget ... so I am happy that you see everyone as equal, but you must be aware of the inherent privileges you are given, from the day you are born, by this society, because of something so 'crazy' as skin color. It matters very much in this world, and the laws that are continued to be drafted reflect that."

"You are being racist by saying that blacks don't have any way of preventing their downfalls than whites. You are saying they aren't equal."

"No, she's saying the world, the reality that black people are relegated to is not equal to the world of white people."

The preceding dialogue is group talk, even though the group had never met face to face and the negotiations were played out one at a time and at a safe distance. The group of women writing on the restroom wall in the English department building at my university were speaking, listening, making room for opinions, disagreeing, and negotiating. They were confronting the issue that Taylor, Gilligan, and Sullivan found the most troubling to deal with in groups: the continuing problem of race. There were at least ten *different* handwritings, maybe quite a few more, represented on the wall of the bathroom stall, and the writing extended over a period of at least a year (Figure 4–1).

These women's talk indicated to me how much students want and need to talk about the race issue. Their emotional reactions, their puzzled comments, and their understanding of perspectives indicated how deeply felt their comments were. But notice as well how they found points of similarity as they took one another's sides: "No, she's saying ..." They used evidence to promote their own claims and to

Figure 4–1　Group work on a bathroom wall

reinforce others. They retreated and advanced, and found common ground as well as difference. They did it in a small group, a virtual group of sorts that changed with the person who entered the stall, but one that operated as all good small groups do: to change and be changed by the social encounter the group provides for. What I included is only a segment of the graffiti on the wall. But all the comments demonstrated the same attempt at conversation, the same need to work through the conflicts presented by the race issue.

The troubling element in their talk was the venue in which it took place. Did these women speak anonymously on the wall because they were afraid to speak of these issues in their literature and composition courses? Did they not hear real discussion of racial issues in their history classes? Were they afraid to voice their opinions where they would be held accountable for them, where in face-to-face talk they'd have to own them? Did teachers stymie the conversations that might begin about race because of their own fears? As Nel Noddings (1992) said, "Teachers are often unwilling even to talk with their students about moral matters," in part, "because they know they are not psychologists and don't feel they have the right to impose their own values on students" (p. 39). Teachers have made similar statements to me when talking about why they have shied away from using a racially sensitive book or essay in class or why they've limited discussion about sexual politics or race relations in their classes. But, as Noddings pointed out, "These same teachers enforce all sorts of rules—sensible and mindless equally—without questioning the values thus imposed" (p. 39).

Although they've been trained to impose rules and the values that underlie them without fear, many teachers do fear being the only voice imposing only one set of values when the values are explicit, such as in discussions of politics or race. Group work helps reduce this fear since it encourages many perspectives on sensitive issues and even on the rules teachers enforce. For me, a teacher of literacy, the women's talk on the bathroom wall represents an admonition, a challenge to make the groups I encourage in the class to be as open and trusting as I hope for them to be, to find ways to bring the conversation from the bathroom stall into the writing classroom.

Out of the Closet and into the Class

As earlier chapters have demonstrated, the process of coming to know, of learning itself, is always dynamic, influenced by the social environment as well as by the task, by the others around, and by the individual. "Since it is always a process, knowing presumes a dialectical situation: not strictly an 'I think' but a 'we think.' It is not the 'I think' that constitutes the 'we think' but rather the 'we think' that makes it possible for me to think" (Peirce, 1992, p. 365). C. S. Peirce, the great late-nineteenth-century American logician and pragmatist philosopher, wrote these words to describe how learning and knowledge happen. He pointed to the way in which the individual learner is changed and constituted through interactions with others. The pragmatists writing on the bathroom wall were figuring out how the "I think" gets constituted by the "we think," how their individual opinions get shaped and altered by others' thinking. When one wrote to another "You are right 100 percent. I am white and only recently (at 39 years old) came to understand that the major obstacle to racial harmony and equity and justice is white privilege," she was exploring connection and the process of change. She, like many of these other women, was linking her imagination to others' imaginations.

The easy classroom pattern of teacher talk–student silence, teacher question–student response is often insufficient to meet the demands of this "I think" and "we think" process that Peirce recommended and the women students writing on the restroom wall practiced. My students and I call the pattern the *Ferris Buehler method* of teaching (from the great teen movie *Ferris Buehler's Day Off*), the deadly space between a teacher's bored inquiry—"anyone? . . . anyone?" and students' even more bored silence in return. It's a practice that is, in Paulo Freire's (1973) terms, a *methodological error*, a mistake in procedure or pedagogical strategy that doesn't serve the end of learning (p. 86). One of my students doing an ethnographic study inquired into the nature of questions in class, creating a taxonomy of types, or the sorts of responses students made, the kinds of questions they asked. What he found was not surprising: questions from teachers and students are rare; they are small and pointed rather than large and conceptual, and their answers are predetermined. In only one case in three days of observing two classes were questions from students turned back to students with another question ("What do you think?" or "Does somebody want to respond to that?"). In no case was a question that was put to a teacher modified by a student's response ("I never thought of that" or "Maybe there's a larger issue here"). Much of class time is spent in neither question nor response, limited as that is. Most of the time is spent in teacher talk and student silence.

*   *   *

As Freire (1973) said, methodological errors have ideological roots. No classroom practice comes without beliefs that underscore and direct it. "To correct them requires more than the insistence on methods themselves. It requires a permanent revision of the ideological class conditioning of the teacher" (p. 88). The roots or methodological beliefs that guide the Ferris Buehler method—or some less dramatic variation of it where the teacher asks, talks, and affirms, and the class nods, questions, and accedes—is based on a model that presumes that the teacher is knowledgeable and the students are ignorant, at least ignorant of the demands of the classroom. To reconstitute this method, teachers must do as Freire asked: look at their own "class conditioning," their own understandings about how people come to know. To have the "I think" and the "we think" work together in a classroom, teachers must transform their classrooms into spaces where the "we think" can operate more effectively, more transparently, more like the women's conversation on the bathroom wall.

The multicultural classroom is a reality. And it's a strength as well. Diversity is what feeds us, what promotes and extends learning. Putting together the new, the different, and the unfamiliar with the old, the same, and the comfortable is a good way to describe the learning process itself, and the classroom group, suddenly, it seems, so variously composed of different ethnicities, races, classes, and origins, presents fertile ground for learning by linking old and new. Yet the differences the multicultural classroom represents present problems as well, where our democratic ideal insists on a myth of sameness: that everybody is the same, with the same chance, the same purpose, and the same background. We ignore difference to preserve objectivity, highly prized in institutions, or to promote fairness. How can we recognize the reality of difference, confront it, and allow it to become the powerful tool for learning that it can be? The reality of difference means that students will come to the classroom with various experiences, beliefs, and opinions about the issues they will confront in their reading and writing. If the small group is a tool for learning in the classroom, these different voices, these different perspectives on sometimes highly charged issues, will be heard rather than suppressed.

*   *   *

bell hooks (1994) suggested that an awareness of multiculturalism has not been accompanied by changed pedagogy. "Despite the contemporary focus on multiculturalism in our society, particularly in education," she said, "there is not nearly enough practical discussion of ways classroom settings can be transformed so that the learning experience is inclusive" (p. 25). hooks argued that we may need to change teaching styles: "Let's face it: most of us were taught in classrooms where styles of teachings reflected the notion of a single norm of thought and experience, which we were encouraged to believe was universal" (p. 25). As teachers examine the implications of multiculturalism for their classrooms, they have to confront their own lack of preparation and experience, the limitations of their knowledge, and their possible loss of authority. These thoughts are not comfortable, and some teachers understandably back away from them. As hooks said, "Many teachers are disturbed by the political implications of a multicultural education because they fear losing control in a classroom where there is no one way to approach a subject—only multiple ways and multiple references" (p. 36).

hooks led a small group of colleagues at Oberlin College in rethinking pedagogy to accommodate the multiple perspectives that cultural diversity in subject matter and the student body presented. She said, "We found again and again that almost everyone, especially the old guard, were more disturbed by the overt recognition of the role our political perspectives play in shaping pedagogy than by their passive acceptance of ways of teaching and learning that reflect biases, particularly a white supremacist standpoint" (p. 37). Although the group struggled, hooks took some understandings from it and from her conversations with her colleagues. She noted that the unwillingness to approach teaching from a standpoint that includes awareness of race, sex, and class is often rooted in the fear that classrooms will be "uncontrollable, that emotions and passions will not be contained" (p. 39). These teachers pointed to their feeling that the classroom should be a safe place; hooks said, "That usually translates to mean that the professor lectures to a group of quiet students who respond only when they are called on" (p. 39). The experience of many students, especially women and students of color, indicates that this kind of neutral classroom setting often does not feel safe at all, and this absence of safety keeps so many students quiet and disengaged in the classrooms they inhabit.

Race and the Group

Although it is increasingly the case that students come from various racial and ethnic backgrounds, my classes remain overwhelmingly white. In a typical writing course with twenty-two students, I may see five students of color sitting in front of me. In graduate courses, I may have one student, if any, who is not white or middle class. African American students and other students of color are sometimes silenced by their minority status in the classroom, especially when racial discussions centered on issues or texts ensue. A teaching assistant in the composition program came to me once, saddened by his attempt at creating what he assumed was a multicultural environment for his writing students, all of whom were white except one. "We were supposed to read King's 'I Have a Dream' speech yesterday," he said. "And then she was absent." The teacher thought he was creating a safe space for talk and a place where his one student of color could have something special to say. But that very fact likely accounted for his student's absence. Without realizing it, the teacher had made his African American student take on the role of expert on the "black perspective" for the white students in the class, and for him as well. It was too big a burden to assume.

Feeling the need to confront racial issues more effectively in her classes, another teaching assistant asked her students for advice about dealing with race in her class. An African American student wrote this:

> I feel race is very important here at UNCG. [A student] stated in class "I'm the only black in one of my classes and the *teacher* and students look to me when a question of race comes up!" If race wasn't an issue this wouldn't happen. The white teachers don't know how to approach Black students, so they are asking. Well, honestly, there's nothing you should know. You already have your opinions, stick by them. OR try to find out from someone else, not me.

This student addressed the minority problem directly. He was another student, not the teacher, not the expert on race relations, and he resented and feared being looked to for "help" with race issues. Notice that the word *teacher* is underlined; he was particularly dismayed by what he saw as the teacher's abdication of authority and responsibility.

"Making the classroom a democratic setting where everyone feels a responsibility to contribute is a central goal of transformative pedagogy" (p. 30), hooks (1994) argued in her book. Although hooks didn't talk much about methods or specific practices that might create this setting, it's clear that the small group fosters just this kind of responsibility to contribute among its members, so the small group needs to play a central role in the kind of transformative pedagogy hooks advocated. "Multiculturalism compels educators to recognize the narrow boundaries that have shaped the way knowledge is shared in the classroom" (p. 30), hooks said, and we broaden and break these boundaries when we learn how to make the small classroom circle the primary unit of our instruction.

The conversation, discussed in Chapter 2, among the teaching fellows who were critiquing Mary Rose O'Reilly's (1993) book, *The Peaceable Classroom*, was also a beginning discussion of racial issues, as the students brought their new experiences in student teaching in multiracial classrooms into the conversation. They saw the differences and the difficulties that present themselves when students come from racially bound and poverty-stricken homes in the "projects," where students' experiences with tragedy—death, violence, and destitution—argue for a new kind of understanding by their teachers. "Why do they need to talk about war?" one teaching fellow questioned, as she commented on O'Reilly's argument. Another responded to her, talking about one of her students who had just dropped out of the school where she was teaching, a school that was 94 percent African American: "He's had the cards stacked against him since day one. First, who knows about his dad, his best friend got killed. A couple days ago he went home, took a nap, woke up and found his mom dead. This is the violence I worry about." A third group member continued, "Maybe if you can keep a kid in school you can indirectly prevent them from being drafted into this quote unquote war that's going on. Domestic violence and all that stuff."

This group of dedicated young women who were soon to become teachers were using the literature they read to explore the most sensitive and knotty problem they would face in their classrooms—the way that poverty, racism, and institutional separation affect students' educational futures. They didn't all agree, but O'Reilly's book gave them a common meeting point and a locus for their talk. The fact that they were to write a review of this book—a review that would be published—gave them a real goal and real work to do so that the negotiations they made were part of a mutual process of inquiry. Reading literature, whether it's fiction or nonfiction, can be used strategically to help students understand new dimensions of old, and continuing, problems.

Using Reading to Confront Racial Issues

When small groups talk about literature well, they pull the cues the text offers to them together with their individual, and then collaborative, responses to their reading. This process mirrors the way that readers unconsciously read when they read alone. One advantage of group work in the context of reading literature is that this unconscious negotiation of text and reader's experience is made overt and explicit as it's articulated in the group's conversation. A reader who silently juxtaposes his or her belief (derived from background and experience) about affirmative action with the plot of Guterson's (1994) *Snow Falling on Cedars,* as my first-year writing student Raymond did, may be unaware of how his or her view of the novel is affected by the connection he or she makes. But when the reader discusses the issue in a group, he or she can see how and why he or she found issues of discrimination at the heart of the novel and how he or she might reconcile what was read with personal beliefs. The group talk allowed Raymond to re-create the path of his thinking and to challenge it. He became a more critical reader because the group allowed him to articulate his ideas and let him find a space to think more deeply about his reactions.

The text can provide students with evidence, support, and a narrative to talk about their reactions to the problems of race and racism, as well as other sensitive issues. A student who might be uncomfortable speaking his or her views on capital punishment, for example, can illustrate or expand on these views as he or she discusses the characters in Ernest Gaines' (1993) *A Lesson Before Dying,* a novel I asked my group of teacher certification students to read in our writing class. This novel, which is about injustice and literacy and the calling of teaching, gives powerful testimony to the connection between crime and poverty, racial injustice and judicial injustice. Students in my class met in groups to decide how they might teach this book and derived lesson plans to guide them. In the process, they talked about the different views they had grown up with about capital punishment and about poverty, the way students might see these issues now, and how individual opinions might be negotiated.

One group member wrote about her group's talk concerning the unit they might teach using the novel:

> I brought my knowledge of American history and my own personal experiences to the reading. I have had the opportunity to read a multitude of different books, ranging from *Roll of Thunder, Hear My Cry* to *Their Eyes Were Watching God* to a US History book. And I've been able to discuss that reading openly, where you weren't wrong, but where your opinion mattered—and if it changed, that was OK too. But some people, we decided, don't have this broad base. We decided to work on history first. I'll bring in stacks of journal articles, history books and newspaper and magazine articles from the 1930s. I would split them into groups and give them topics to consider, and these topics will of course connect to what we'll find in the novel.

Another group member created two fictional students, very different from each other, to discuss the problems reading literature together might present. She ended:

> I think that even "Bonnie" and "Tommy" could overlook each other's differences, if they were given the opportunity to share their ideas and become part of a literary group.

Choosing texts. The literature that students read in their groups should be chosen for its richness, its ability to engage, and its appropriateness for grade level and classroom curriculum. These are the considerations teachers take into account in choosing any text for classroom discussion, and these considerations should remain the same when a work is selected with racial issues at the center. Teachers should choose these works for interest and for their connection to other stories and to the students. But as in all literary works where sensitive topics come up, teachers need to be careful not to deny these topics, the rhetoric the characters use, or the characters themselves. bell hooks (1994) gave the example of the white female professor who "is eager to include a work by Toni Morrison on the syllabus of her course but then teaches that work without making reference to race or ethnicity..." (p. 38). One teacher once told me proudly that her students could read Zora Neale Hurston and "not even deal with race."

In selecting texts for small-group discussion, then, teachers need to deal honestly with the kinds of issues that will come up in discussion and to make room for these discussions to occur. Teachers send an important message when they integrate texts by familiarly canonical writers with texts written by writers of color and with characters whose race or ethnicity is a central focus of the literary work's theme. Once this kind of integration occurs, students in groups are likely to consider factors of race, as well as class, ethnicity, gender, and politics as they read all their texts.[1]

One important consideration in choosing texts for small groups is to find texts that provide a variety of perspectives. But just as important is to let groups locate these perspectives as they work. When my teaching students worked with Gaines' (1993), *A Lesson Before Dying*, in their groups, they chose different approaches to teaching the text on the basis of the different significances they had located when they were reading the novel. One group chose to focus on the strong women in

---

1. For an insightful discussion of race and racism in canonical American literary works, see Toni Morrison's (1992) *Playing in the Dark: Whiteness and the Literary Imagination*. In her book, Morrison illuminated the racial preoccupations of writers like Cather, Poe, Melville, Twain, Faulkner, and Hemingway and thus provided new paths for teachers to take in discussing the multicultural dimensions of these commonly taught works.

the novel and the way women work for change. Another group created a series of lessons that asked students to concentrate on language and the message that language is powerful. Still another group developed a research project that investigated capital punishment and located information on the Internet about the number and the ethnicities of people on death row in the United States. As they presented their lessons to the class at large, other groups were taking notes, considering how to use the various approaches and opinions they heard in their real classrooms.

In this class, black and white students talked in their group not only about the book and the racial prejudice that informs the novel's themes, but also about their racial experiences, their segregated or integrated schools, and their feelings about racial issues. "Busing is finished in Charlotte," one African American student told her group. "Did you read that? And now the schools will get just as segregated as they were before. I was in school there. I know." Another shook his head. "I don't know what I feel about that. So many parents seem to want it this way." Their serious discussion about their pasts and the cultural present was played out against the need to create a lesson plan and with the story as a kind of shield for them to use to work through their complex reactions to racial tensions and to racial injustice.

Whatever the text, when groups work with literature in their small groups, teachers need to allow for a variety of activities so that the racial conversation can emerge through the activity they're completing together. The work itself creates a safe space for honest, caring discussion to emerge.

Using Writing to Confront Racial Issues

As a way to introduce a reading or a discussion or teaching issues, I often ask students to write about memories of the first time they encountered someone of another race. When I ask student groups to write about this, they rarely have trouble beginning. Sometimes we have talked in small groups about racial issues as they've come up in a reading or in something that has happened on campus, but just as often we haven't talked much together before they write this response. When they finish writing, and I tell them to take only twenty minutes or so, they look back at their responses to find a word that captures the feeling of what they've written. They decide how they'll share their response with their small group—reading aloud, explaining, or talking about the word they've chosen. The conversation in the groups is soon lively. I share with them my memory. I've written it, I tell them, in an essay about race and Southern women. I tell them how much it helped me to write it; sometimes later they come and talk to me about it and about their own memories. Following is an excerpt from my story about Marie:

> When I was eight or nine, I had a friend whose name was Marie. Pronounced with a drawn-out short *a* and a long long *e*, it sounded beautiful when someone spoke it, the name of a French queen. When I visited my grandmother's house in New Orleans, Marie would come to play. She was the daughter of my aunt's cook and she was black.
>
>   ...I remember someone coming in, my grandmother's friend, and taking my arm, setting me upright. Marie and I stopped laughing abruptly, and the friend said something stern to me about behaving "like a lady." Nothing much happened after that; no scenes, no racial discussions. But Marie's visits dwindled and then stopped. It has taken me over thirty-five years to understand that I was being taught a lesson that day.

My students nearly always react the same way to this small story. They ask, "What happened to Marie? Did you ever see her again?" They can hear my sense of loss as I retrieve the experience, and they are saddened by my telling them that I saw Marie rarely after that, even though I visited New Orleans every summer for many more years. In their small groups, they return to their own stories and begin to talk more deeply about what it meant to them to "discover" race or racial prejudice as young children.

I've realized that my small classroom groups provide safety for the deeply felt exchanges that sometimes emerge from these memories. Unlike the large classroom group, the small group provides an intimate and relatively unexposed position from which to offer opinions and experiences that may be difficult to voice among the twenty-five or so other students in the class.

Several years ago, I conducted a series of workshops at the University of New Hampshire's summer writing program. In one workshop session, I asked participants, experienced classroom teachers, to write about their early memories of encountering someone of another race. Like my young students, and like my own memory, these teachers' reflections centered on loss, a kind of vague regret. "I don't know what happened to Joe," one wrote about her Hispanic friend from first grade. "He must have moved." "I remember going to her house and seeing all the pictures of a black Jesus," another wrote. "I guess I just stopped going over."

The similarity in these responses, from black and white students alike, feels like a beginning. If groups can read one another's stories about their friends of different colors and find connections, they initiate the process of understanding. My students have been able to read Toni Morrison and James Baldwin, as well as Nathaniel Hawthorne and

Eudora Welty, more deeply because they've talked in their group about their memories of how black and white relationships develop or get stunted. And because of their reading and their talk together, they've come to new understandings of the loss of connection that underlies our vexed notions of race in this culture.

Gender and the Group

On the surface, the problem of gender seems not nearly so dramatic or difficult as the issue of race. Although many public schools in the United States remain racially segregated, most are integrated sexually. Young men and women talk freely, it seems, about issues of equality and access, and women's voices appear to be as strong as the male voices in their classrooms. Yet a wealth of reports since the 1990s indicate that serious problems remain. The 1990 American Association of University Women (AAUW) report (1990) suggested that "our school systems fail to meet the needs of girls. . . . The wealth of statistical evidence must convince even the most skeptical that gender bias in our schools is shortchanging girls—and compromising our country" (p. v). As books like Mary Pipher's (1994) *Reviving Ophelia* and Maureen Barbieri's (1995) *Sounds from the Heart* have demonstrated, the middle school years present particularly difficult challenges for young women, where they begin to mature in a culture so saturated with sexist messages.

Despite gains in women's education and women's authority in the workplace, a large gap remains in terms of gender equality, and students' perceptions that "everything is all even now," as one of my female students once said to me, only add to the problem. Everything is not even. Studies of educational opportunity and practice at all levels indicate persistent sexism and discrimination. Isaiah Smithson (1990) reported in the Introduction to *Gender in the Classroom* that women receive twenty-eight percent fewer grants and sixteen percent fewer loans when they enter college than men do and are more likely to withdraw from school due to financial problems. While veterans' benefits aren't taken into account in eligibility decisions about financial aid, food stamps and Aid for Families with Dependent Children that many women receive are counted as income. Only ten percent of college and university presidents are female. These statistics barely scratch the surface of the factors that contribute to the university as a "chilly climate for women," the phrase from the 1990 AAUW report (pp. 1–2). Smithson (1990), following the line of much other research, noted that the discrimination women face in university settings only continues traditions established in kindergarten, where girls and boys are often presumed to have different skills, especially when it comes to math and science and where books and activities continue to have "sexism as their subtext" (p. 3).

Smithson concluded from these facts that "American education does profound, lasting, psychological damage to many of its female students," (pp. 6–7) giving them incomplete histories of their sex, limiting literary reading to a canon "canonical in part because of its projection of male fantasies hostile to women," subtly suggesting that some careers and options are not open to women, and allowing men to dominate in classrooms. Smithson suggested that the classroom only follows the larger society in its continuing undermining of women's equality in the culture.

Clearly, it's important to combat the traditions and assumptions that prevent women from achieving equal status and opportunity in education. Classroom strategies that concentrate on creating more equal spaces for women can go a long way toward rethinking these traditions and assumptions. Frances Maher (1985) wrote that a pedagogy that would attempt to hear the voices of women and others whose perspectives have been ignored must be "collaborative, cooperative, and interactive" (p. 31). It should stress cooperation and involvement over competition. It should move away from the lecture format and toward more "democratic" classroom practice. It should, it seems clear, learn to use the small group effectively. The group can make all students in the classroom less anonymous and more embodied, an important step in understanding how gender plays a part in language and learning.

Breaking the Anonymous Woman's Silence

One way that it's clear how different the classroom is for men than for women is the new popularity in the college classroom of email lists or listservs, where students talk back and forth about ideas from reading or comments about writing in an anonymous, or semianonymous, way. Many of the teaching assistants in the composition program at my university have found that their female students like the listserv conversation for the way it liberates them from their physical selves. "Nobody looks at me when I write," one young woman wrote to her instructor. "This is the first time my voice is as loud as everybody else's. I can get my words in too," said another. "And I can be anonymous and still have a voice," wrote a third woman. For these students, many women and some men who fear the exposed position in a classroom where everyone seems to be staring at them, the electronic conversation has distinct advantages. If it's set up to do so, the listserv can become a small group in itself, mirroring the sort of connected, mutually active, and supportive conversation that good groups engage in when they work.

As beneficial as these listserv or email groups might be for their ability to free students to talk to one another without exposure, they carry disadvantages with them as well. Women who can raise their voices only when they're anonymous or invisible to others don't necessarily speak more effectively or loudly when they are in real, not virtual, groups. Teaching assistants have reported their disappointment that the good conversations they read online often don't transfer to classroom conversation. Students in face-to-face talk, whether in small groups or in large-class talk, relapse into the patterns they have become familiar or comfortable with in their years of schooling. For many women, this means that they remain tentative, silent, or simply accommodating.

A group of students (Figure 4–2) exchanging papers in a composition class I observed showed how differently males and females can assume authority and voice in their small-group settings. In the class, students provided copies of their essays to each group member for discussion. The essay they'd written was a narrative about growing up, and the teacher was interested in their openings and how they'd organized the time of the story. The teacher had asked them to comment on time and the opening in their comments to one another. The following excerpt is my transcript of their conversation. After the first identification of gender, I assigned names to each group member to make my reading

Figure 4–2 Group discussing a student's essay

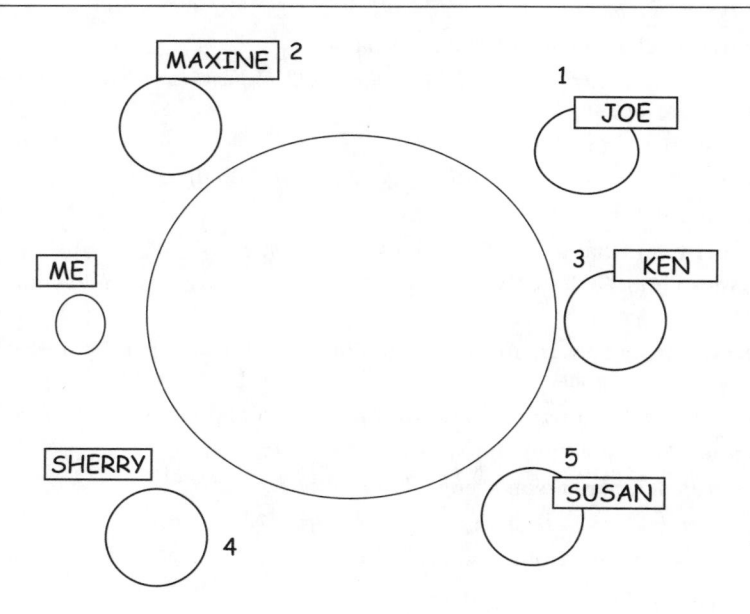

easier. Member #1 was Joe; #2, Maxine; #3, Ken; #4, Sherry; and #5, Susan. In this conversation, the group concentrated its attention on Joe's essay:

Joe to **Ken** (*gesturing*): Let her read it. (*to Maxine*) You've got to help me.

(*They read silently for a minute, and then they all begin to talk quietly. Joe and Maxine are closest to me and also the most active group members. Joe writes as Maxine comments.*)

Joe (*to Maxine*): What's your name? What did you think? (*laughs*)

Maxine: Different. It's very—unusual. You have (*long pause*) a way with words.

Joe: I've been using them all my life.

(*She laughs; Ken and Sherry join in. They aren't dealing yet with the direction to consider how time is used in the essays, but instead are responding to general considerations of the piece.*)

Maxine (*looking at Sherry*): Are you all talking about time now? (*then to Joe*) It's good, I like it.

Ken (*to Susan*): I don't see how much time you're covering yet in your paper.

Susan: I realize that.

Joe (*taking notes, talking to Maxine*): Give a little background.

Maxine: Oh, what did we come up with? (*long pause*) So, what are we supposed to be doing?

Joe to **Sherry** (*reading a comment she wrote on his paper*): Yeah, but what did you see?

(*Sherry speaks inaudibly.*)

Joe: What's that? (*to Ken*) What's her name?

(*The group begins to talk as a whole about time and how their essays have opened using narrative. Joe nods suddenly.*)

Joe: Ok, so if I move this—

Susan: This is a paraphrase. But it's good that you do that.

Ken: He needs to make connections.

Joe: Between what to what? I will, I will. (*He writes.*)

Maxine: I understand what you want. But you have to explain it in your own words.

Sherry: You might want to put it in your own words (*long pause*) because when you begin your paper—

Joe: But you didn't write that down. How am I supposed to know? (*laughs*)

Maxine: You didn't bring it to any conclusion yet.

Joe: Write it down. I won't remember.

(*The groups begin to break apart again and talk together in pairs.*)

Ken: I'm going to try out. I probably won't make it though.

Sherry: You should try out. (*smiles*)

The talk may sound fragmented in its retelling, but it was accompanied by lots of gesture and expression and intonation that completed the questions, extended the talk. Reading over the conversation, you can easily see the patterns of accommodation, support, interaction, and assertion that characterized this group's work. The women in the group for the most part supported and extended Joe's statements, encouraging, gently critiquing, and making suggestions for change. The quiet authority of the women in the group was made use of by the man in the group whose work got most of the attention. The females in the group allowed the group's work to proceed smoothly, but there wasn't much discussion of their own writing except for the terse exchange between Ken and Susan. As my experience with groups has shown me, women too often allow the men in their group to control the group's direction and to receive most of the help and attention the group can offer. They acquiesce to the group's leader, and they become quiet, almost anonymous in the group setting. The young man who kept asking "What's her name?" merely pointed out the obvious, that the women weren't present enough to be remembered individually.

In *You Just Don't Understand,* Deborah Tannen (1990) described the conversational styles of women and men by suggesting a pattern of dominance and support that male-female conversations exhibit. These roles of actor and receptor, Tannen argued, are not simply given but "created in interaction." But, "if men seem to hold forth because they have the expertise, women are often frustrated and surprised to find that when they have the expertise, they don't necessarily get the floor" (p. 125). In the preceding small-group discussion, men and women acted out of the roles of actor and supporter that they had been taught and no doubt rewarded for. The men didn't exhibit any intention to dominate; it happened within the context of the interchange. Women accommodated and stayed away from direct confrontation. Yet, as Tannen (1994) noted in *Gender and Discourse,* "Women's inclination to avoid conflict puts them at a disadvantage" in their conversations with men, who often use conversation as contest and expect resistance to their talk (p. 11).

Women's silence, or anonymity in the classroom group, often serves as a protection, and moving from silence to speech is sometimes fraught with anxiety for them. As Taylor, Gilligan, and Sullivan (1995) noted, "Girls and women learn it may be worse to speak . . . unless you know there's some chance to be heard" (p. 158). The group's ability to break into girls', and others', silence is one of its great strengths and also one of its liabilities, for the ability to speak depends on trust, especially when women talk with men in groups or anyone whose status inherently gives them power. "Coming into relationship across significant differences requires both intellect and feeling" Taylor, Gilligan, and Sullivan said (p. 158), yet the relationship of thought to feeling; that is, the belief that feeling is *connected* to thought at all, has always been the subject for a lot of academic wrangling. ("This isn't a *therapy* group," a professor told me dismissively in describing the rigors of his class.) Collaborative methods that allow women to begin to speak as well as listen, assert as well as accommodate, can begin to work toward the goal of trust, but only if thought and feeling are both seen as critical elements in learning.

Maureen Barbieri's (1995) account of her teaching in a small private girls' school in Ohio illuminated girls' conflicts and strategies as they connected their lives inside school to the culture outside their academic environment. Barbieri used these girls' experiences and their reflections to argue for a collaborative, deeply involved teaching method to prevent young women from falling into the trap of silence and acquiescence that so much of the culture around them praises them for. Barbieri noted that in her classes "the girls often like to work together in small groups, choosing pieces to read and talk about from class sets of short story collections" (p. 56). Barbieri recognized that young women's sense of identity is often "deeply rooted in their perceptions of relationship," and they use relationship itself as a strategy for learning.

Barbieri (1995) quoted Taylor, Gilligan, and Sullivan, who wrote that "the knowledge about relationships and the life of relationships that flourish on this remote island of female adolescence are ... like notes from the underground" (p. 24). When girls share their ideas in groups, they bring ideas from the underground to the surface, learning to tell stories from the "remote islands" and thus bring these islands closer. Barbieri recognized that her past as a voracious reader who never talked about her reading in a group in school was limited. Her passion for reading—"there were periods when I read a book a day—I was insatiable"—went underground with no encouragement for it (p. 67). And, she said, "I can't help but wish things had been a bit different. For now I believe that it is not only in reading but also in writing and talking about books that we come to define who we are and what it is we hope our lives will be" (p. 67). Writing and talking help people define themselves and their goals, Barbieri said. This sense of sharing that's so often missing from the work students do in class is just what group work insists upon. Especially for young women, who are often so reticent to speak and so often ignored or disparaged when they do, the idea of sharing in a group is essential to be able to "define who we are and what it is we hope our lives will be" (p. 67).

When groups negotiate power and authority around their awareness of gender issues, inevitably what has counted as "normal discourse" shifts. When a woman takes on, or is given, a position of authority and control in her group, inevitably the way group members talk to one another changes from patterns they may have been more comfortable with. Men sometimes complain of women with such authority in the group "talking too much" or "dominating" when, as Tannen's research shows, they seldom talk even as much as fifty percent of the time. When groups learn to accommodate different discourse styles more easily, their own discourse expands. Later meetings of small groups who've successfully confronted gender issues, as well as other issues of difference, often exhibit new conversational patterns among all the group members, as they've assimilated new speech patterns and accommodated their own to others'.

Using Reading to Confront Gender Issues

"How many of you in this class have read *Heart of Darkness?*" I once asked a graduate seminar in Theories of Reading. Every student raised his or her hand. Five men and eight women had all read the book. "How many of you have read *Little Women?*" They laughed as they looked around the room. Every woman in the class had read the book. None of the men. We extended the conversation to include other works. *The Hardy Boys, Batman* comic books, *Gone with the Wind, The Awakening.* We talked about what the gender difference in reading might mean. Do males read books assigned in school and not much outside of school? Do females read "boy books" and "girl books," but do males not read "girl books" unless they're assigned?

There's been a lot of research on the differences in the way men and women negotiate the texts they read. Judith Fetterley, in her (1978) study, *The Resisting Reader,* argued that women must read from a male perspective to accurately read books with male characters and male themes at the center. They must *immasculate* themselves to read, Fetterley said, and so are able to find meaning in texts like Joseph Conrad's (1993) *Heart of Darkness,* where the only female characters in the book are unnamed and the perspectives on conquest, civilization, and escape are at least as gendered as they are universal.[2] It may be that one reason women score higher on standardized tests of reading competence is their ability to read *outside* their gender, to remake the experience of reading so that they can participate in what Louise Rosenblatt (1982) called the *event* of making meaning of the text. In 1978, Fetterley was calling for an expanded canon, a curriculum that consciously used texts written by women, so that female readers could find their own experience and ideas sometimes reflected through a lens that didn't

2. Sandra Gilbert and Susan Gubar's studies of women's reading and writing in *The Madwoman in the Attic* (1984), Elizabeth Flynn and Patrocino Schweikart's *Gender and Reading* (1986), and Lynne Alvine and Linda Cullum's *Breaking the Cycle: Gender, Literacy and Learning* (1999) are all good sources for further study on the significant relationship between gender and reading.

require such gender bending. By the beginning of the twenty-first century, canons and curricula had altered to accommodate many more texts written by women and writers of color, as well as by writers of both sexes and many ethnicities who confront issues of sexuality and sexual difference. This conscious effort on the part of teachers to include such texts has strengthened the reading experience for women and for men.

Still, as the discussion in my graduate class illustrated, men seldom read texts that appear to be *women's* books. If women have learned how to immasculate themselves when they read Ernest Hemingway or Herman Melville, men have not become comfortable with *emasculating* themselves when they read Kate Chopin—or Louisa May Alcott. Several years ago, in another seminar, my students read Toni Morrison's (1988) *Beloved.* They worked in groups to discuss the language and the themes in the novel. I had been so involved with the story as a tale of the horrors of slavery that I had not considered the gender implications of the book until one group reported on its effect on them as readers. In one part of the novel, the character Paul D. gets "house fits," a feeling that he has to escape from the closed-in environment of the house where the magical Beloved, her sister, and her mother live. He keeps moving back and away from the center of the action until he's in a small outbuilding. One man in the class spoke of his reaction to the novel as having "house fits." "I couldn't find myself, I kept feeling on the margins of it all," he explained to the class. I wouldn't say that Morrison's novel is a *woman's* book, but part of the point is that the male characters are made marginal, since slave society made them so. My student couldn't read *as a woman* and so he couldn't find his place. The rest of his group were all women, and they talked about how different their reactions were, how they picked entirely different scenes to talk about. The group came to an understanding of how their own gender gave them different insights into the gender considerations and the major themes in *Beloved.*

Part of the work of small groups in discussing reading is to consider the varying reading experiences individual group members take from their reading, including gender. Differences in reaction, in understanding, and in opinions about value are often connected to the gendered expectations readers bring to texts, and group work can aid readers in expanding their perspectives, as well as give them ways to account for their reactions. When males in a class are able to talk about having "house fits" if they read work that puts them on the margins, as a book like Louisa May Alcott's (1994) *Little Women* might, they begin to consider how they "read" other situations, the conversations in which they engage in small- and large-group discussion, their reactions to personal stories, the way they assign value to what they read and write.

Carolyn Heilbrun (1990) wrote that women have always read with a double consciousness—as women and the masculine reader they were taught to be. "Might not men gain now," she asked, "by learning to read, not with a double consciousness but consciously as men in relation to women?" (p. 31). When men and women read literature from lesbian or gay male writers, some find their experience represented and others learn how to expand the representations of experience that they begin reading with.

In my one American Literature class, students chose a novel to read together and report on to the class at large. In part, this assignment was designed to allow students to read a long text in a survey course where most of the readings were excerpts or shorter pieces (chapters from Ben Franklin's, *Autobiography*; four short poems by Phillis Wheatley). I chose the novels with an eye toward their gender and racial consider- ations as well, hoping students would, through their talk, consider the cultural dimensions of the work they read and their varying reactions. Student groups chose novels like Charles Brockden Brown's *Wieland*, Harriet Wilson's (1983) *Our Nig*, and Harriet Beecher Stowe's (1880) *Uncle Tom's Cabin*. Their work allowed them to talk about racial and gender inequities, the treatment of male and female characters, and their reactions as readers to the rhetoric the novels employed. "I think we all learned something new about each other and how we looked at Eliza and Uncle Tom," one of the Bluebirds who read *Uncle Tom's Cabin* claimed.

Expanding their reading list to include more works by women and writers of color is no guarantee that women or minorities will find themselves represented or feel more powerful as speakers and writers in the class. But combined with a teaching practice that makes the small group the locus of conversation about texts, fosters the goal of developing consciousness of individual perspective and the ability to take on others' perspectives. In the American Literature class, the group found the issues it wanted to raise, and the teacher's opinions or ideas about the work became secondary.

Using Writing to Confront Gender Issues

Because it feels less direct and thus less exposed, women sometimes prefer writing to speaking in a composition class. In the small groups in one freshman composition class, I observed an early group meet- ing where each group decided how it would present material to the class. One young woman, Andi, volunteered to record. "As long as I don't have to stand up in front of the class," she said, "I'll take all the notes." The young woman sitting next to her shook her head and said, "No, you've got to speak sometime. I'd rather just take notes too."

Writing within and for the group can become a way of not speaking, and the women in my classes often eagerly take on the role of writer-not-speaker. But, as the exchange between these two women shows, students will negotiate the roles they take on, especially if the teacher sets some agendas for collaboration in the groups early. I began the semester, as I do each semester, by talking about various roles in the group and declaring that roles would shift (see Chapter 5, Maxim #2). Everybody would be a writer; everybody would be a speaker at some point in their many small-group interactions, I had told them. No one would use writing as a shield against speech.

When all students write in a group, they learn much about individual writing style and voice. A collaborative journal, where each group member writes reflections or ideas on a topic and comments on the reflections of other group members, provides a strategy for teachers to use to help students see the various kinds of discourse that individuals can produce in the free-flowing form of an ungraded, unevaluated journal. This kind of collaborative journal is easy to accomplish electronically. In addition, when students begin to comment on pieces of one another's writing, they often initiate conversations about style that have gender considerations underlying them, and the talk about matters like amount of detail, use of story, and use of punctuation becomes a way for the men and women in a group to think about their own writing and their response to others' ideas and drafts.

One important way to make writing a tool for the discussion of gender issues is to use prompts that ask students to respond to a gender issue and then to use the writing as a springboard for talk and for further writing. For instance, following is an example of two students in a small group, one female and one male, writing about an excerpt the group had read from David and Myra Sadker's (1994) book on gender and education, *Failing at Fairness*. The differences in perspective are clear, and, because each group member shared the writing, a fine discussion ensued about the relationship of the reader to the text and the importance of gender in understanding, and reacting, to the text:

1: As far as girls not getting their fair chance to be heard and receive attention. I disagree with. In my experiences, girls have the opportunity to speak but they don't. Most girls aren't assertive in the classroom, they just sit there and take notes. . . . I cannot blame the educational system for it. At school, all students are treated fairly, and it is up to the girls whether they want to represent themselves as assertive or weak.

2: I didn't notice it until we started talking about it in class. Girls or women get treated different than men. Most girls are taught to sit back and wait until everyone has stopped talking, basically to be "ladylike." Meanwhile, the boys are being taught to stand up and make noise, get all of the attention.

In one of my classes where there is a lot of discussion I noticed that most of the men and most of the black women talked. 95 percent men talked— 95 percent black women talked and only 1 white woman says anything (one white woman out of about 20). That surprised me a lot.

The students began a discussion of how race plays into the issue of gender, about their own classes, and about their backgrounds. The group moved on to talk about their next writing assignments and the way that they might use their discussion to help frame their writing about the gender roles in a group of essays the class was reading together. Their writing, and the discussion of it, led both the men and the women in the group toward new kinds of awareness about their own learning. Their ability to talk honestly and perceptively about issues of gender was surprising to them, and empowering.

In her 1999 book on writing, *Remembered Rapture: The Writer at Work*, bell hooks wrote about the power of language as a communal event:

> We write because language is the way we keep a hold on life. With words we experience our deepest understandings of what it means to be intimate. We communicate to connect, to know community. Even though writing is a solitary act, when I sit with words that I trust will be read by someone, I know that I can never be truly alone (p. 13).

Language itself is inherently involved with life. It's social, as hooks argued, even when we write alone or for ourselves. hooks' comment about writing as a bridge between one's self and another that lets her know she's never "truly alone" shows how much writing depends on an *other*. One reason, then, for the small group that engages with one another's writing is to let students see to what extent writing is the way to keep a hold on life, to connect, to explain, and to not be alone.

* * *

I've talked about race and gender, and I've not talked about the other issues of difference—the enormous problems of class and economic disadvantage, differences in ethnicities, in sexual orientation, and in physical and mental ability. But by using these two large areas of difference and discrimination, I think I've made it clear how to break and broaden the small-group circle to encircle other kinds of diversity as well. Exploring difference is about relationship. Taylor, Gilligan, and Sullivan (1995) wrote near the end of their study of adolescent girls, "To hold difference and sustain hope requires us, moment by moment, to hold steady, to stay with ourselves and each other, to continue to learn how to speak in the presence of profound silences" (p. 173). The group lets us continue to speak, to stay with one another and ourselves, and thus to hold onto hope.

The Culture Circle: Diversity in Action

In his work with the dispossessed and the illiterate in many Third World countries, Paulo Freire (1984) discovered and refined a method for fostering the sort of critical negotiation and accommodation that the best groups, in and out of school, work toward. Reading the world, Freire said, always precedes reading the word, and for this reason Freire's program of literacy begins with the worlds of those he teaches: "Words used in organizing a literacy program come from what I call the 'word universe' of people who are learning, expressing their actual language, their anxieties, fears, demands, and dreams" (p. 37). The subjects for study, the vocabulary employed, and the ideas explored come first from "the people's existential experience" (p. 37), not from the teacher's. Of course, students have an investment in ideas and subjects that derive from their own backgrounds and experiences, as well as a sense of budding expertise. But even more important, these students learn to rethink their own experiences as they tie them to others' and articulate them in new contexts.

The process of literacy for Freire is a growing consciousness of the relationship between the individual and the world around him or her. His or her *culture circle* is a small group that comes together to tell stories, draw pictures, connect ideas, and learn to read the world and the word in new ways. Beginning with their own words, or their own metaphors, or their own drawings, the circle becomes aware of how it enlarges and reshapes itself as each member talks and listens. Even more important, the learners becoming literate in the culture circle begin to see themselves as the subjects of their own learning, the actors in their worlds, and the meaning makers in the acts of literacy they engage in. As one of the participants in Taylor, Gilligan, and Sullivan's (1995) study said to her interviewer, "Speaking helps me by just realizing, because when I answer these questions, I realize things that I did not even picture" (pp. 128–29).

The culture circle talks, writes, and draws from out of its experience and thus creates meaning for its small world within the group and the larger world that the group is a part of. The culture circle thus represents the best kind of small group, a group of mutually interactive and supportive members who each nurtures his or her literacy by connecting it to all the others' literacy. The generative words for the culture circle, the words that express deeply and mutually held meanings, become the words the group uses to reinforce its connections and to find relationships between and among them, especially when members are of diverse backgrounds and with divergent interests.

Freire (1984) described one culture circle he visited in a village on the coast of Brazil, where he observed the way the circle was working together as they were learning to read and write:

We visited a Culture Circle in a small fishing community called Monte Mario. They had as a generative word the term *bonito* (beautiful), the name of a fish, and as a codification they had an expressive design of the little town with its vegetation, typical houses, fishing boats in the sea, and a fisherman holding a *bonito*. The learners were looking at this picture in silence. All at once, four of them stood up as if they had agreed to do so beforehand; and they walked over to the wall where the codification was hanging. They stared at it closely. Then they went to the window and looked outside. They looked at each other as though they were surprised and looking again at the codification, they said: "This is Monte Mario. Monte Mario is like this and we didn't know it" (p. 67).

This small epiphany demonstrates the process of learners' seeing the connection between the world—the environment and the actions—in the fishing village and the world the members of the culture circle created through their representation of it. They were learning the power of representation—including language—to express and illuminate something about *them*. And this kind of growing consciousness that occurs as the small group talks and writes and imagines is exactly the kind of *critical thinking* that we wish to nurture among our students who are becoming increasingly literate within the context of the work we all—teacher and students—engage in together.

At the University of New Hampshire (UNH), I used the strategies of the culture circle to suggest how critical consciousness can be reinforced in the small group. I had spoken to the large group of teachers early in the week about Freire's program of literacy, the importance of language, the uses of the group, and the need for personal action and belief. I had used his terms—*generative words, codification, culture circle*—to explain the process of literacy development and Freire's insistence that learners themselves must be the subjects in their own learning. In a workshop session a few days later, in a class of ten or so teachers who were investigating the relationship between art and writing, I asked them to create a codification, to draw the place where they grew up. We used crayons and newsprint paper, and the teachers suddenly became learners again, children finding the best colors to make their representations. A few asked questions: "Do you mean the house?" "Could it be more than one place?" But most were content with the purposely vague direction I had given, and they set to work.

After fifteen minutes or so, I asked them to step back, look at their drawings, and then write three words that described something about the picture they had drawn. I divided them into small groups of three or four and asked them to talk about what they had drawn. Their pictures were various, as you might expect. They drew houses and yards. They drew streets and people. Some perspectives were from close in—with a front door or a window dominating the scene; others were perched

Figure 4–3   Three teachers' responses to the culture circle task "draw the place where you grew up": (A) exterior perspective; (B) interior perspective; (C) birds'-eye perspective

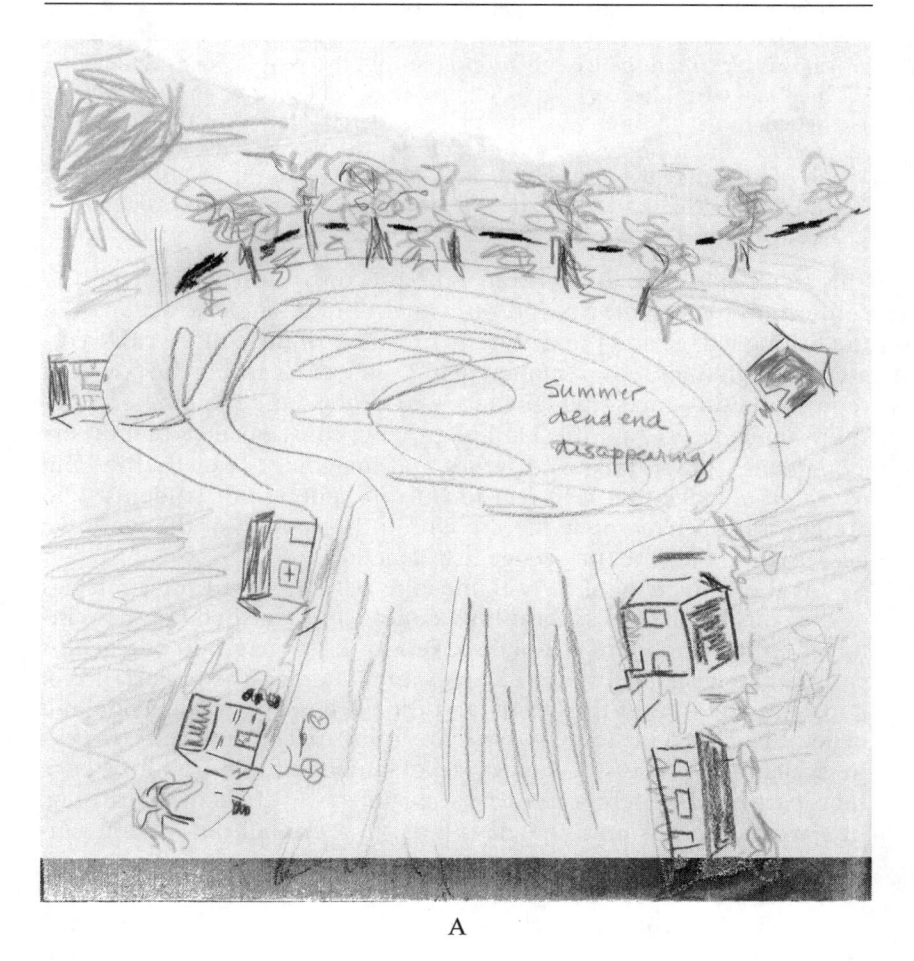

A

far away with the house a dot on the landscape. A few drew interior scenes; one drew only trees; another, a grid of streets and buildings (Figure 4–3).

The words varied as well, but many were repeated: *safe, small,* and *warm* appeared several times. Many words were similar, words that had to do with comfort or size or sound. In the pictures in Figure 4–3, you can see some of the patterns the pictures evoked, and the groups talked about these patterns as they described their pictures to one another:

Figure 4–3   (Continued)

imaginative
comfortable
solitude

B

how some drew interior space and others concentrated on the out-
doors, how some put themselves in the picture and others had no figures. Some took a bird's-eye view of the scene or created a map; some
focused on a window or a door. As they talked about these patterns,
they began to tell the stories the drawings evoked, and when the group
came together to show their pictures to everyone else, the stories led to
others—about siblings and food and reading and emotions—that led in
turn to discussions of the importance of past to present and about the
role of environment and friends to an attitude about home.

The group—the culture circle—discovered patterns that linked
them, as well as differences that helped them see one another in new
ways. They created *generative words,* words they could use to evoke stories. I told them how the stories they told could be written and linked to
form what Freire called the *popular library,* the literature a culture circle
produces that becomes a text to read. If we were in a class together, I
said, we might then add to this library other texts with similar themes or
generative words, and your learning about the past and home would be

Figure 4–3   (Continued)

protection
intense
fun

C

extended to include more perspectives that would be linked to those we had uncovered together. This process, enacted by the group of teachers at UNH, illustrates the way that a small group can work to find new meanings and, most important, can find its own voice and authority in the process of learning.

Creating the Culture Circle in Small Groups

Students don't need to draw pictures to enact the process of learning that Freire's work calls for. But pictures are a provocative way for students to discover the power of representation and to uncover their own generative words. In the courses I teach for preservice teachers and in first-year writing courses, I often ask students to draw their elementary schools or their high schools. In other courses I've asked students to draw their workplaces or homes. Still other student groups draw graphic representations of their writing processes or the plot of the novel they've read. As they describe these drawings and comment on them, they discover what they think as well as what they share. And they find new ways of linking their perceptions as they discuss the thematic patterns in Nathaniel Hawthorne's work or talk about ability groupings in high school. Their representations and the words they use to describe them become generative, provoking new perceptions and new stories. Difficult issues of class, gender, and race can be discussed in the framework of shared generative words. And students are at once both the authorities, as they describe their representations, and the learners, as they respond to other representations.

Whether students in a group begin with drawings, begin with pieces of their own writing or other texts, or begin with a question or a problem, the idea of the culture circle represents the process that makes group learning potentially so powerful and important in classroom work. It's the process that one young teacher was looking for as she wrote in her journal about her frustration with her student-teaching experience:

> These kids couldn't communicate, and the idea of dialectic, at least in a classroom, was foreign because it was banned from their usage. Get into groups! Now not later! Groups of three not four! Don't talk! Ok, now you can talk! Be quiet! Sit down! Are you on task? (You have to watch them every minute or they'll pull something.) What are you doing? What did you say? Speak clearly! Shut up! I left student teaching dazed and confused, but probably no more confused than those students. I found it to be "metaphorically impossible" to constantly be the person whose job it was to silence, to frighten, to threaten and at the same time to nurture and lead. Do you understand what I mean? Everything about that school was "counter dialectical," and it nearly drove me insane to try and change that, but I still feel that it is of earth-shattering importance that we *do* change it. Collaboration, to me, is not just "group work" or "coauthorship." It is a way of acting and interacting in society that is needed right now, not just for the future of literary scholarship but for the future of the planet, of humanity. Am I taking this too seriously? I really don't believe so.

This teacher wanted to make her group work become a culture circle. She needed to help her students create a place where they could engage in the "dialectical" process of learning, where each was responsible for him- or herself and others, where a student was a teacher and a learner, where change had a chance to occur. She was looking for a way to make group work real in her classroom.

When it is a culture circle, group work becomes a way to have the imagination work. The imagination is not something reserved for the art classroom or the creative writing workshop. Ann Berthoff (1981) used Coleridge's idea of the imagination to define it as "the forming power of mind" (p. 54). Group work, when it's the kind of interactive and dialectical activity that the young teacher longed for, becomes the forming power of *minds,* the ways in which individual ideas get tangibly altered and improved by the swirl of small-group conversation into which they're dropped. Like the imagination, the power of minds forming ideas together is already there within the group, waiting to be activated. If it's regarded as natural and usual, the way that meaning gets made, teachers might find group work to be the central activity of their work in classrooms.

The next, and last, chapter offers some suggestions, some blueprints for action, for making groups the central work in the classroom.

Chapter Five

Blueprint for Action
Making Groups Work

Books about classroom methods often fall into the trap of providing theoretical support and rationales for the strategies they advocate and shortchanging the practical contexts that will determine whether or not these classroom methods have a chance of success. This book has attempted to suggest methods with a host of examples and illustrations, as it's explored the difficulties in groups and the possibilities for overcoming these difficulties. And it's argued, persuasively I hope, for an agenda that puts group work at the center of an organizational plan in developing curriculum. In this final chapter, I examine some of the practical realities about how to put groups in place in classrooms and how to help them function most effectively to become what Ann Berthoff (1981) would call the *speculative instruments* of learning.

The plans and suggestions that follow should serve as a blueprint, rather than as a manual, for making groups work. A blueprint is really just a suggestion with numbers, with its lines challenged and changed as the actual building gets under way. The structure intimated by the lines of the blueprint is filled in by the architect—by the reader of the blueprint's text—and the lines and measurements facilitate not only construction, but also the architect or reader's imagination, as the structure begins to take shape inside the mind and outside in the world. The advice I offer should be like this blueprint; a plan that teachers can use to confirm and stretch their own thinking on the basis of how they imagine the classroom structure. The ideas I advocate come from my experience with dozens of groups I've worked with over the years. But classrooms are various; teachers and students interact in a host of productive ways. And so I offer practical discussion, hoping that teachers will find ways to have these practices fire their imaginations as they draw the small circles that will become the groups in their classrooms.

Maxims for Breaking into Circles

In the opening section of *The Making of Meaning* (which is subtitled *Metaphors, Models, and Maxims for Writing Teachers*), Ann Berthoff (1981) wrote about her use of these three terms as ways to "grasp the implications of theory" and thus to stimulate the imagination. "Maxims," she said, "can make theory accessible; they provide a way to keep our speculative instruments handy." Although maxims are set down as imperatives, they should be understood in more imaginative ways, by "encourag /ing/ us to explore what is implied" (pp. 7–8). Maxims are instructive, in other words, if the reader unpacks them, applies them, and works out their implications for him- or herself. The maxims that follow are offered in this spirit, not merely as exhortations and certainly not as rules, but as tiny fables that suggest possibilities for teachers in their work.[1] I have only four maxims to offer:

1. Make group work organic.
2. Teach people how to work in a group.
3. Make membership in a group permanent.
4. Make the group's work real.

Maxim #1: Make Group Work Organic

The teacher walks into his or her classroom at the beginning of the year or the semester, pleasantly greets the students, and hands out the syllabus for the term. The teacher's voice sounds loud and clear in the words of a syllabus, even if he or she's not particularly conscious of it. It's revealing, for example, if a syllabus begins with rules rather than with ideas. The syllabus voice sounds bored or excited, challenging or rigid. And this voice conveys lots of qualities that students use to help

---

1. Berthoff's (1981) maxims for writing and teaching can serve as aids for the establishment of groups as well. They are as follows: (1) Begin with where they are; (2) how you construe is how you construct; (3) to understand is to invent; (4) elements of what we want to end with must be present in some form from the start; (5) to the teacher the simplest and most general appears as the easiest, whereas for a pupil only the complex and living appears easy.

   Using these maxims, teachers can consider both the makeup of the groups they help create and the kinds of activities that group work will foster most effectively. (See pages 3–12 of Berthoff's work.)

them think about how they will write, how they'll behave in class, when they might ask a question, and how often and if they will ask for a conference; in short, how they'll conceptualize their roles as students in the classroom.

If small-group work is a significant part of the classroom work, as I've argued that it must be, then the syllabus should clearly signal this importance in its message and its voice.

Examining my American Literature syllabus. Following is the beginning of a syllabus from an American Literature course I taught:

What Makes Literature American?

The aim of this course is to explore how writers in the New World began to shape a new literature and how that literature contributed (and still does) to the forging of a national identity. We want to examine the American literary tradition and the elements in the newly emerging American culture that made it so radically different from the European tradition it derived from. By necessity, we'll be highly selective (though you'll be encouraged to read work we won't have time for in class), so we'll be looking for patterns as we read and write about these works. And we'll be reading a variety of genres, letters from women to family and friends, diaries and journals of explorations, songs of Native Americans, narratives of Africans brought to this country, legends of Hispanic peoples. We hope to emerge with a sense of the richness of the colonial, revolutionary, and new national experience that led to an American literature. We'll write often in and out of class, producing several short papers and at least two longer ones. You'll make one oral presentation, and your group will make a class presentation as well. We'll meet in small groups often, and a lot of the work of the class will center on the discussion that emerges in your group. Your consistent attendance is therefore crucial to your success in the class.

Evaluation: I won't typically give grades on individual assignments. At midterm, I will give you a gradesofar. I encourage you to talk with me at any time about your grades and your work. You will keep a portfolio of your work and progress that will include a selection of your written work and presentations as well as reflections on your writing. Your final grade will be based on your work and participation in your group, your written work and journal, and your final portfolio.

Week 1: Introduction to the course: What makes literature American? Read up to 22.
　　　Group talk: comment on response on two visions (handout)
Week 2: In class response: Mr. Emerson speaks: an American literature
　　　Group: comment on Emerson
　　　Short history lesson: puritans, explorers, Indians, and pilgrims
　　　Group: famous figures: becoming culturally literate

The syllabus continues for three or four more weeks, not for the entire semester, which is an indication of how much the class group would determine how quickly we'd move. They would also help determine what we'd read, as I asked questions to gauge their interest and experience.

This syllabus beginning revealed to the students who read it the importance I place on group interaction and responsibility, letting them know that the group work they would accomplish would be an integral part of the work of the course. In the syllabus, you can see that I talk about the aims of the course in terms of the work students would accomplish together, and then signal how much of the work would come from the small groups they would work within. When I described how they'd be evaluated, I talked about the group's role as part of my evaluation. And in the week-by-week portion of the syllabus, I indicated places where the group would work together. I used nearly the same words in my freshman composition syllabus and in that for the course I teach for teacher preparation students. In every course I teach, I always schedule at least two group meetings during the first two weeks in the semester. As students read this syllabus with me (I talk about the syllabus and our goals during the first meeting when I hand it out), students come to understand the importance I place on their group work, an importance I stress both in terms of participation and attendance and in understanding course goals and activities.

*   *   *

The syllabus is one way to signal the central position of groups in the classroom. As groups get under way and the class begins to establish its pattern of breaking from the large circle of the whole group into its smaller circles and back again (or from small circles to the large one), the organic role of the small group is reinforced by the work within the group. The activities and tasks students accomplish in their small groups should connect to the work of the whole class (an easy way to ensure that this happens is by asking groups to "report out" to the class) and to course goals and concepts. Groups connect course goals and their activity in the group when they all work on the same problem or the same kind of assignment. Students in groups might all engage the same question (What does Emerson mean by a *mere thinker*? When have you been *man thinking*?) and learn how different or how much alike responses might be when groups report to the class at large. They might all be responding to initial paragraphs of drafts (perhaps of papers that have developed from the preceding question) or all writing on the same issue (writing together in a group fosters a deep sense of engagement when the stakes are low; when the writing is ungraded and engaging).

All the groups in my American Literature class, for example, read novels their individual groups had selected and all prepared presentations to make for the class. The novels were different, and the methods for presenting them varied interestingly, but the class felt a common bond in the activity itself, even as each group was reading different novels and finding different approaches to make the novel come alive for the students who had not read it. Noting the differences in approach, in presentation, and in the novels themselves became a lively large-class discussion after all the groups had accomplished their work.

When they made decisions about how to approach their novel, the groups did so in the context of "course concepts" almost without thinking of these concepts. We had spent lots of time talking about the way early American writers grappled with the environment that surrounded them, how they used religious faith and pragmatic reality to make sense of this environment, and how they used their personal and public lives to create a voice on the page. These concepts became a part of the presentations students made. If course concepts are considered when teachers develop small-group activities, students will use these concepts as they approach their work.

Part of making group work organic within the classroom structure is to allow classroom time for students to meet often in small-group settings. Time is no small issue. In a class where there might be only forty minutes of class instruction (the situation in many high school English classes), the small group may seem like an intrusion, or it may simply get squeezed out by other demands. One significant advantage of the recent "block scheduling" in many high schools across the United States is that it facilitates the use of small groups, since class periods lengthen. (The significant disadvantage of having classes meet for only a semester rather than a full year, which happens in some forms of the block schedule, is another matter.) Whether a class meets for an hour and a half or for forty minutes, group work can be accomplished successfully only if students meet often enough to know and trust one another and to build together a repertoire of information, ideas, and experiences. If a class meets three times a week, some of this time each week should be devoted to small-group activity. Students shouldn't go more than a week without coming together in their group.

Groups don't have to meet for the whole time period in a class. The time spent in groups should vary according to the task and how the task fits into other activities. Ten minutes of writing one paragraph together, finding a good quote from a text, planning an outline, or trading drafts serves the purpose of getting useful work done while nurturing group connections. Sometimes the groups may need to meet for most of the class time, if they're preparing a presentation for the class or commenting on group members' drafts. It's not always necessary to call groups back into the larger circle at the end of the class, although many teachers feel the need for some kind of closure on the day's activities. When groups record and reflect in the group folder at the end of a group session, whether or not they report to the class at large, they get a sense of work accomplished and progress made that's crucial for groups to experience.

Envisioning how a class *moves* in any week's worth of work is a good way to think about how groups contribute to the course. Teachers decide how to begin a class each day; some of these days they might ask students to move into their small groups at the beginning of a class period and then move back to the larger group. Some days the class will remain in one group; some days they will remain in their small circles. The key is to have a rationale for the moving back and forth—and to exercise it.

Maxim #2: Teach Group Dynamics

In her journal, one of my students commented on her experience as a student teacher beginning to work with groups. She pointed out the difficulty of asking students to engage in an activity they had little positive experience with:

> I got to be on the "teacher" side of the experience during student teaching. What I observed was that students didn't know *how* to work in groups. They had no training, past experiences, or models to follow in cooperative group learning. As my teacher and I visited each of the groups, most of our instruction was not on the assignment but rather on how to divide the tasks and then bring together their efforts into a cooperative product.

Too often, teachers assume that the act of putting students into groups will result in good group interaction. But the truth is that students who've had little chance for the kind of cooperative, collaborative endeavor that good group work requires often have few skills to bring to the circle once group work gets under way. You might have noticed in some of your classroom groups a silence once the work begins, almost a sullenness from some group members, who'll usually be the ones to say something such as "What did she want us to do?" Teachers who fear their groups' going off task often are reacting to groups who avoid their collaborative tasks by talking about everything else or who fall into individual meanderings, drawing or reading other work, or sleeping. Many of these students have simply not been taught how to engage in group work.

In *Making Learning Happen*, Jeffrey Golub (2000) offered some helpful strategies for making a small group's interaction successful by practicing the skills group members must use as they work together. Golub said these skills include the following:

Speak loudly.

Ask appropriate questions as well as answer them.

Contribute and respond, but do not dominate the discussion.

Act as a group leader.

Help the group reach agreement.

Stick to the topic.

Recognize the significance of nonverbal communication.

Paraphrase and summarize.

Draw the group back to the topic.

Check perceptions about the meaning of statements and ideas.

Initiate discussion.

Seek people's opinions, especially of those who have not been talking.

Clarify ideas.

Motivate other members of the group.

Brainstorm for ideas (p. 86).

Golub contended that group members don't begin to know how to use all these skills, and he provided a host of activities designed to foster group cooperation and collaboration in problem solving, sharing ideas, and writing. These pregroup activities were designed for grades six through twelve, but they can be useful beginning strategies for older students as well.

*   *   *

It's clear that students need help in learning how to listen and speak, accommodate and assimilate, and lead and follow. How might teachers provide such "training" in group work? Like other problems in our culture that get translated into the classroom, the lack of conversation and collaboration in our communities and families is related to students' misunderstanding about how to work and play in a classroom group. Some students never sit down with their families for a meal and never share the day's experiences. They don't express their ideas or listen to siblings' or friends' ideas, in part because there seems to be less and less time for this sort of reflective activity. They don't see in their neighborhoods examples of people working to solve problems or repair something together. It's become a commonplace that we all seem more and more isolated from one another, working alone at a computer screen, driving alone in a car, and crossing the street to avoid passing a stranger. We are at once becoming more interdependent and inter-connected, as the population expands and technology radicalizes our notions of privacy, and more separate as we fear these encroachments on our individuality and autonomy.

Our students feel this strange dichotomy too. It seems even more important then, than in years past, to help students learn to speak and listen, to accommodate, to work together through problems and ideas, and to develop a sense of self that can come only through seeing the self as one among others—the way life is lived.

Assigning roles. In my groups, I begin by describing the roles and the titles individual group members will take during their work together. Every role shifts during every group meeting. The president has no chance to become a dictator; the recorder doesn't take dictation for long; the reflector pulls ideas together for the public only on occasion. Not every student has an assigned role every time the group meets, but every student will assume every role at several points during a semester's work.

The president. The president's job is to keep things moving, to make sure everybody gets a chance to offer ideas, to watch the time and help set the pace, and to make sure the work gets done. I name this role *president* rather than *leader* for its ceremonial title. Leaders emerge in the group, and they are not always the people who have the title of president for a given day. The president has leadership thrust upon him or her but can exercise it however he or she wants—including to have the group's work proceed smoothly.

The recorder. The recorder does just that: keeps a record of what the group does with its time. If the group work is to present reactions to a quotation from a story or to respond to a character's action, the recorder takes notes on these reactions so that someone in the group—not nec-essarily the recorder—can present them. In fact, I often tell the recorder that he or she can decide who will present to the class at large, since so often recorders don't like the job because they're always the ones to speak. When the group is planning a project, the recorder makes notes the group keeps for itself. If there's something to be turned in to the teacher (a plan, questions, responses), the recorder collects them. Sometimes there's nothing to be written; the recorder decides if notes are necessary.

The reflector. I recently added this role to the small-group circle. Although all students are reflectors—commentators and responders to whatever the group engages in on any one day—the reflector's assigned task is to look back at the work and consider what's been accomplished and where the group needs to go. This role is especially useful when a small group is planning a project or a presentation. When my American Literature students met in groups to discuss how they'd present the novel they'd read together to the class, the reflector was the person who gathered his or her impressions of what people had decided to do: "So we think we want to begin with a movie clip and then wait for reactions from the class, right? The movie is a good way to get everybody involved right away. Some people will have seen it, and they'll help us when we start talking about Uncle Tom." This kind of summary and reflection creates a kind of group solidarity, as everybody in the group agrees that a film clip is a good idea and—even more important—agrees about why it is. The reflector steps back, gathering up the threads of the conversation and then showing what he or she's gathered to the group. He or she may write for the group and may lead the group toward decisions, but his or her role is more of a mirror of group accomplishment than either that of the recorder or that of the president.

*　*　*

When I describe these roles, students ask other questions about how the group will spend its time, how often their roles will shift, how much people should talk—all the issues that good groups depend on members to know. A useful strategy to help students find their roles and help them in their conversations with one another is to have volunteers act out a group session for the entire class early in the semester. Sometimes I take a role to get them started, but usually students perform with little prodding. I give them a line from an essay, or a letter to the editor, or even a beginning writing assignment, and then I ask them to model the work they might do in their group. Modeling bad group work is effective too. In fact, students are adept at becoming bad group members, since, unfortunately, they've usually had experience in being in a bad group. I take only ten or fifteen minutes with this role-playing exercise, but it's another way to provoke discussion about how people interact and how each person might be responsive to others and responsible to the group.

Once groups get under way and begin to feel a sense of shared responsibility, the assigned roles sometimes disappear. Students naturally undertake the process of figuring out tasks and how they will get their work accomplished. But as the group is forming, and for some time after that, roles help students perform the functions necessary for collaborative effort.

Maxim #3: Make Group Membership Permanent

I am a little hesitant about this maxim: make group membership permanent. I know that students sometimes wish they could move around from group to group and, as they tell me, "get to know other people in the class." I know that sometimes, especially if you set up groups randomly the way I do, group members aren't always the best matches—too many quiet people, too many bouncy ones—and that you can resolve these personality mismatches if groups are shuffled every so often in a class. And time makes a difference: in high school, for example, where students are together in a class for an entire academic year, it might be productive to move people around in groups after they've been together for twelve weeks (a third of the school year) or so.

But I tentatively stand by the idea that groups should see themselves as permanent small units in the classroom circle. First, as this book has argued, groups can succeed only to the extent that they foster trust. For people to voice opinions, to share writing, to react to a topic, or to explain a quotation, they have to feel that others are listening and *believing* in them. That's not too strong a word to use. I speak more effectively to an audience disposed to believe I have a right to speak and something to say that they might use than I do to a group of people who regard me with suspicion or boredom. More than that, when I'm listening to someone, I have to believe in the person who's speaking and trust that he or she does have something to offer or contribute that I might find useful or interesting. The group needs this kind of interactive belief; it needs this trust. And trust takes time to nurture.

A typical college semester lasts no more than fifteen weeks, and often only thirteen weeks of real class time. Students in college classrooms meet one another only two or three times a week. They often don't know one another at all before they enter the classroom, and many in first-year classes are just learning how to negotiate the demands of college life. The permanent small group in their English class becomes a place where students can get to know other people, share worries as well as ideas, and hear themselves articulate opinions in a relatively small, and safe, environment. The trust that can flourish when groups know they will stay together for the term allows writers to become willing to share their drafts, readers to offer suggestions and real opinions, speakers to learn to listen, and listeners to learn to speak.

When I give each group its bird name, I help establish this *permanent* group identity. I picked birds because my first-grade groups were named after birds, and I wanted students to think of all their primary school memories of reading groups as I talked to them about their groups in our class. But as I discovered with all the many incarnations of Redbirds and Eagles and Parrots and Flamingos, the groups begin to take on a character, an identity that they establish in part because they're given a name. When my daughter was a first-year student at the University in Chapel Hill, she came to visit my first-year writing class and stayed with us for the hour, moving into one of the bird groups. A few weeks later, she was walking on her own campus when she was greeted by one of my students. She didn't recognize him at first. "You know me, Kate," he said. "I'm a Pigeon!"

Students define themselves in terms of their groups, often writing phrases like "Eagles Forever" or "Falcon Pride" on the informal notes the recorder keeps. These little epigraphs reinforce the group's trust and connection. I don't think it could happen as well or as easily if groups switched membership. One first-year student wrote this note on her final portfolio:

> I have never before been a part of such effective group work. I have loved watching our group mature and build trust. We each brought a variety of experiences and beliefs to our work together. I have learned a lot from my Eagle friends....I have learned from this experience the importance of maintaining the same groups over a period of time and creating opportunities in class for frequent group interaction. Go Eagles!

If a teacher wants to accommodate students' desire to meet and talk to other groups and still retain the primary bird group, he or she can create scenarios where groups form for short periods and then disperse. For example, if an assignment calls for students to react to one of six quotes, a teacher might form groups according to each individual's selection of a particular quotation. I have sometimes asked students from one group to be emissaries to another group for a day to discuss an issue or a problem that group has been investigating and to hear what another group has to say about it. These methods mix up the permanent group without disbanding it and give students an opportunity to hear from and speak to others outside the increasingly safe small space of their own group.

The group folder becomes both a record of a group's activity and a way to underscore and promote group negotiation and identity. The group folder is just that: a folder where the group keeps the record of what it's accomplished in any one meeting. The group knows it's doing work because this work is visible in the folder. This way, no one person is responsible for keeping all the groups' writing and planning; the members simply put it in the folder, which I most often collect at the end of the class meeting. And I respond to groups by writing in the folder as well, reacting to their plans and commentary and suggesting avenues for the group to explore next time.

The kind of trust that an ongoing, and stable, group can provide for writers—especially beginning or hesitant writers—is evident in the comment that Bill, a first-year student, wrote to me to accompany the final draft of a paper he had worked on with his group:

> Dear Hepsie,
>
> Famous Last Words about my paper. Well, I think it turned out okay. I was able to write a lot more than I expected. I had a very rough draft on Monday for my group meeting and they gave me the confidence I needed to continue. When I started writing again all the thoughts just kind of fell into place and the gaps closed.

Maxim #4: Make the Group's Work Real

Many of the comments from students in previous chapters describing their fears and dislike of group work attest to the need for the group's work to be real. Students complain of group work with foregone conclusions, having to engage in a process that teachers had already decided the outcome for. When students mention the uselessness of the time spent in groups, they talk about performing group tasks that clearly had no effect on the rest of the agenda in the class or about activities that were put in a group setting only to fulfill a perceived need to meet in groups.

So what do I mean by *real*? Primarily, I mean that the group accomplishes something that I didn't know the answer to beforehand and something that individual class members couldn't accomplish as effectively were they doing it by themselves. As a teacher, I have to think as carefully about the tasks I give to groups as I do to the writing assignments I make or the novel I choose. A task such as filling in the blanks on a worksheet is usually not a good task for groups (although there could be good reason for such an activity). Students sometimes say that in their groups they always let one person do the work because this person did it best or quickest. They often talk about group activities such as filling in the blanks. And they have a point: if the task doesn't require negotiation, it's probably best accomplished by individuals or the whole class together.

Peer response and evaluation is a common small-group activity, and in this book I have talked about how useful it is for students to share and respond to one another's drafts of assignments. But unless students know and trust one another and have a pretty clear idea of what might constitute effective writing, they won't see this task as any more real than filling in the blanks. Teachers are often frustrated by student responses to drafts that say something like "nice idea" or "add some detail." But many students are afraid of their own reactions and fearful of offending the writer; in addition, they don't believe their own reactions matter much to the writer. After all, most times the small group isn't giving the "real" grade. For the peer response group to be effective, each group member needs to feel that he or she is writing to the audience of the group and that the group can help the writer in thinking about what he or she might want to add or change.

In my teaching class, I gave a group assignment to teach a grammar lesson. We had talked about the teaching of language as the teaching of grammar, I had modeled a lesson about restrictive clauses using a Dorothy Parker short story and some discussion of the story's male-female themes, and they had considered their own fear of grammatical problems and their worst grammar flaws. Their lesson was a culmination of all this discussion.

One student from the Eagles group wrote an assessment of her grammar lesson in her portfolio at the end of the semester:

> Our grammar lesson is an excellent illustration of our work together. One day Mary was discussing some of her struggles both with a paper and with life when she began to sing the "nobody loves me...guess I'll go eat worms" song. That comment sparked Donna's imagination which led to the creation of our cans of mud and worms. Brandy and I used our analytical skills to figure out the grammar problems and how to fix them. I am amazed how much grammar I learned in our group simply because it was a comfortable environment where I could ask questions and try new ideas.... Our group sometimes was a little disorganized, which I felt showed through in our presentation. We had discussed the use of non-standard grammar as a stylistic device but somehow we got mixed up when delegating parts of the presentation, and that important idea slipped through the cracks. Slight disorganization was certainly worth the benefits of our work together though.

Liz's comment illuminates the process this successful group went through: talking together, listening for ideas, and planning their presentation. She noted the "slight disorganization" of the final product, but she was proud of their insights and what they were able to bring to the class's attention as they presented their grammar lesson.

Another student wrote about how her essay on a novel changed because of her group work:

> I usually don't like getting into groups because my grade would be dependent on it, and I usually ended up in a group that was not as dedicated as me. I'm sure you've heard that one a thousand times....I really enjoyed the group I was a part of this semester. I liked the fact that I was able to get to know my classmates better than I normally do in a class. Our group was fun, and I feel we genuinely wanted to help each other. We had good brainstorming sessions when it was time to discuss topics of essays or proof our drafts. One time in particular

I remember was, we were discussing Gaines [*Lesson Before Dying*], and Jerome and I had a wonderful discussion about the character of Jefferson and the power of words in the novel. That is what I was writing my paper on, it was awesome to hear his opinion and use it in my paper.

Jennifer, a first-year student, also talked about how her confidence in speaking out and exploring ideas grew as a result of finding the work of the group engaging and real:

We did a pretty good job on our presentation. I think this was because everyone in the group had a good understanding of the essays and shared their thoughts and ideas freely in our meetings. I really enjoyed sharing my insight and different ideas about what we read. In fact, I feel so much more comfortable with sharing my ideas with my group. I was even a little bit nervous about this aspect of the class in the beginning, but now I am comfortable with sharing and contributing.

Teachers Talk Back: Questions About Groups

A teacher once stopped to talk to me after a workshop I had given on reading. The conversation turned to groups, and she laughed. "I've got a question for you," she said. "What do I do about Max?" She described her student, the class clown, who derailed every group he was in with his games and jokes. "People never talk about the real students in the class, the ones who make it so tough to have a group." I've talked often to groups of teachers about the value of groups and about how to make group work productive in a classroom. If they have a chance, teachers always raise good questions about the realities of the practices I advocate. The questions I end with are real questions written for me by five teachers, from both high school and college classrooms. Their questions overlapped one another when I looked at their lists, and, perhaps not surprisingly, they echoed the questions that have surfaced again and again in the conversations I've had with teachers and students. I think they're a fair representation of the kinds of questions teachers need to have answered as they begin putting groups to work for them effectively. My responses are certainly not definitive answers, but they are reflections on what's worked for me and for the teachers I've worked with over the years.

What Do You Do About Personalities?

What to do about personalities ranks first among the questions teachers ask me when they're considering how to use groups in their classrooms;

it is the question that concerned Max's teacher when she stopped to ask me about the problems with groups. It's the question repeated, in one form or another, on every one of the lists from the teachers who wrote questions for me. Teachers are right to worry that an individual can ruin the group's work by demonstrating—through silence, talk, or action—his or her lack of interest in the group's endeavor.

Part of the answer to this problem, and there's no doubt that in some groups it is one, comes in assigning roles. With recalcitrant group members, a teacher may need to pay special attention to that group to make sure roles are indeed switching. Even more important is to make sure that a teacher devotes some time—after class, during the small group meeting, or in a scheduled conference—to talking to the group as a group. A good time for this kind of conversation is when the group is readying a presentation or commenting on one another's drafts. This talking and listening in on a group gives help to students who may be unsure of their roles or harboring resentment about a too dominant personality or a too uninvolved member. Once the teacher sees problems with individual group members, a talk with the individual student may be the best solution.

If a group member is too dominant, two students vie for dominance, or a group member is too uninvolved, the small conference in combination with an individual talk can often resolve some of the problems, particularly when roles are continually shifting in the group. In some cases, although this rarely happens in a semester-long class, group members might need to shift. I would avoid simply moving the offending person around, however, since the person who's taking too much control, for example, is often simply going to transfer that behavior to another group. Better in this case would be to find a natural time for regrouping everybody: at the midpoint of the term or at the beginning of a new unit.

This strategy can help teachers confront the student who doesn't contribute his or her share to the group's work, who allows the others to take the lead in planning, writing, presenting, and contributing ideas. If groups are given a measure of control over their work, they themselves often work out the difficulties. A student commenting on his group's class presentation wrote about the issue of the nonworking group member:

> Due to a general disorganization within our group, our presentation did not go as smoothly as possible. Circumstance limited the number of people in our group to three; one Canary dropped the class altogether and another had to leave town for personal reasons. This made for some stress within the group; but for the most part, I think we did fine concerning this. About 15 minutes before class, we had an argument about the workload we each bore; the lack of communication had

caught up with us. And about five minutes before we were to present, Paula, who had been gone, came into class unaware that we were presenting.

One of the ways students deal with workload is to pick up the slack, as these students had clearly done. Yet, their assurance that they could talk about the process and their contributions to the presentation—and in fact had to since final reflection on group projects is a significant part of my evaluation of their work—let them feel less anxious and aggrieved about their workload. Since much of the resentment students feel about group work, and a nonworking group member, centers on the issue of evaluation and grades, teachers have to be careful about how they make group evaluations.

How Do You Set Up Groups for the First Time?

If you look back at Chapter 1, where I described the first meeting of my freshman composition class, you'll see how I usually set up groups. The main thing is to make the small circles quickly, in the first or second class meeting, so that students immediately see that their group work will be an important and ongoing part of their responsibility in the classroom. When a teacher sets up groups this early in the year, he or she has little or no idea of the personalities or strengths of the individuals placed together in a group. And this is crucial too. In *Lives on the Boundary,* Mike Rose's (1989) powerful account of struggles of students at the edges of academic achievement, the educational "underclass," he uncovered the truth that students respond quickly and sometimes irreversibly to teachers' expectations for them. "Students will float to the mark you set," he found (p. 26). If a teacher knows a student to be quiet, or domineering, or chatty, or a quick study, and attempts to match students in a group on the basis of these qualities, he or she will likely program students to retain these behaviors in the groups chosen for them. As Rose pointed out in his moving description, students are quick to notice what teachers think of them. All the students I've ever talked to about their first-grade reading groups knew precisely whether they were in the "best" group or the "slow" group no matter what title they had and no matter whether it was ever mentioned to them. I remember myself in first grade feeling sad for the Yellow Birds because they were the slow readers.

Assign groups quickly, then, before you have much of an idea of who your students are, at least who they are in your classroom. Some teachers ask students to count off numbers and then put all the students with the same numbers together. Typically, I group students together as they're sitting. I don't worry if two friends are together; in my experience, knowing another person in a group carries more advantages than detriments. I try to call the students' names as I group them; it's one way for me to learn names quickly and for them to learn their fellow group members' names too. I always begin by telling each group to get acquainted, learn each others' names, talk for a bit, and then begin the activity for the first group session. The first activity should be something that doesn't require too much exposure—a reaction to a quote, the beginning of an essay, or a piece of in-class writing.

What's the Optimum Size for a Group?

I'm not sure there is one good size for a group. Part of determining size will depend on how many students are in the classroom and how large the classroom is. Students need to be able to move themselves into groups easily (something you can't take for granted in many classrooms where sometimes desks are bolted to the floor or where there are tables instead of chairs). They need to be able to hear one another speak, and in small classroom spaces where there are many groups, hearing is sometimes a real difficulty. But generally four to six people is a good size for the small circle. Three students seems to put people into roles too easily, and one person becomes the mediator for the other two way too often. And when groups are larger than six people, it's hard to give enough space to everyone's contribution, and the problems with hearing and physically moving chairs get worse.

How Do You Evaluate Groups?

Groups should be evaluated often. When groups keep a process folder—with notes and plans for projects, reflections on the work they accomplished as they examined drafts, and outlines of the comments they make to the classroom after a group session has ended—it's important for me to comment on their work. Looking at one of these group folders, I see notes such as "Think about the next question now." "Did you get to Tess's draft late? You didn't talk about her opening." These kinds of short in-progress comments let students in the group evaluate their effectiveness even as I evaluate it.

When a group makes a presentation, I write a long commentary on the group's work, noting both how the presentation has succeeded for me and how individual members contributed to it. Following are excerpts from my commentary to the Bluebirds, a group of first-year writers who had presented a discussion of the rhetoric in an essay by Toni Cade Bambara that the class had read. In my opening paragraphs, I spoke of the presentation as a whole: "Dear Bluebirds, Your presentation was successful because you talked honestly and specifically about your reactions to the essay as well as its primary elements, and you got the class involved in thinking through rhetorical elements of the essay with you." I then spoke of their interaction: "You seemed to work pretty well together too, though you could have integrated each angle more effectively if you had moved back and forth in your conversation a little more." After a discussion of their strategies and their effect, I spoke of individual contributions: "Tanika: I like the biographical and cultural background you bring up but I wish you had gone a little with the real story that occasioned this piece. Be careful about not reading everything. We lose your voice when we can't see your face clearly." This kind of individual and group commentary reinforces the idea that students are individually responsible for the work of the group as a whole.

As part of their group work, students write reflections at midterm, after presentations, and in their final portfolios that describe their contributions to their groups. These reflections are usually honest portraits of themselves, even when they feel they've contributed less than they might have. One student wrote of her part in a presentation: "I wanted to make a few other comments here and there, but every time I opened my mouth about something I hadn't written down, the words deserted me. To be honest, I tried to hide the memory loss with things that did intrigue me in the story, and I know I was a little rambling."

My final letter to students, which I write at the end of the term after I've read their portfolios, indicates how well I think they've participated and contributed to their group's success. My syllabus has shown them that group work is a part of their final grade, and my letter addresses this significant part of their classroom performance.

With all these moments for evaluating and commenting on the group's process and progress, students seldom feel that they have not been given credit for their group's collaboration or that others have been given credit unfairly.

How Do You Convince Students of the Benefits of Group Work?

Some students are already willing to be convinced that group work is beneficial, and others are recalcitrant; both reactions are based on past experiences with classroom groups. You've heard in this book lots of comments from students who resist group work, mostly, I would argue, because their groups and activities within them hadn't been well thought out by the teacher. The best way to convince students that group work has benefits is to let them see these benefits in their own writing and their own classroom voices as they become more confident and more skillful in communicating. The same thing goes for convincing department chairs or principals of the benefits of group work. More alert, engaged, skillful students provide a powerful testimonial for small-group efforts.

How Do You Help Students Do Effective Peer Review and Response?

The question of how to help students do effective peer review and re-sponse comes from teachers who are using groups to accomplish writing workshops, and the writing workshop in a small group can be a fine way to get students thinking imaginatively and productively about their own writing. But students generally aren't prepared to do this kind of work right away. The first thing, then, is to begin with tasks that don't require as much confidence and skill as responding to a draft of a classmate's paper usually does. Writing together—a paragraph, a bit of dialogue, or a response to a letter—is a good way to begin the process of understanding the demands of audience and of writer. Everybody is equally invested; no one feels spotlighted; no one feels uncomfortable with critique. Later, writers might want one question about their draft to be answered. They might underline a line that seems problematic or particularly good to them, and readers can respond to these places. If everybody in the group brings just their opening paragraph, they can share ideas about how they've decided to begin. I think it's important, in most cases, for writing assignments to be designed both to provide flexibility for individual writers and to foster a sense of community. The instruction "Write about some topic you're interested in" won't allow students to see their work *in terms of* others' work, and this is essential for students to be good readers and to expand their writing horizons. My first-year class wrote its first essay on the power of names. I even gave them a working title: "A Myth About Me." The essays differed widely in tone and content, but, as students read one another's drafts, they found common ground for discussion and saw the wide array of possibilities that opened up for them as they read.

How Much Should the Teacher Be a Part of the Group's Work?

For me, the question of the extent of the teacher's involvement in the group is maybe the most difficult to answer and the most important to consider. In part, this is because of my personality. I tend to take center stage easily, and I get so interested in a group's conversation that I have to stop myself from jumping in too often to comment. For some teachers, it's less of a strain to sit in a group awhile and just listen. I think the answer is to be as involved as you need to be to help the group's work proceed smoothly. Sometimes, early in a semester, it's good to provoke a group who's having trouble communicating well by making yourself part of the group for a few minutes, modeling with your responses the kind of talk the group itself might begin. Some teachers make themselves part of one group for a class meeting and the next meeting move to another group. Others move among groups, stopping to listen or to comment and then moving on. I have tried both strategies. For me, it works best to stay out of the group's talk as much as possible. Generally, when it's close to time for the group to disband, I move among the groups to find out how they've done, where they are, and if they're ready to discuss what they've accomplished with the class at large.

How Should Groups Keep Track of Their Work?

I've spoken of the group folder, the file the group keeps of its work in progress and its reflections. The folder is a useful way for groups to keep track of what they accomplish and to use this information in later meetings. I generally collect these folders at the end of each class meeting, so that no one student in the group is responsible for it. Occasionally, I look through the folder and make comments when I see something especially interesting or when the comments, reflections, and plans seem too general or sparse. A real advantage of these folders comes in final evaluation, where I ask students to include a discussion of their work in groups as part of their final portfolios. Students draw from their group folders as they comment on what they've done well and how their group has worked together.

Is Group Work More Appropriate for Certain Students? Certain Courses?

Group work is appropriate and necessary for all students at all levels. Certain courses may fall more naturally into small-group patterns, largely because of their physical contexts. The biology lab where there is one microscope to every three students presents a clear opportunity for group collaboration as a teacher designs an experiment or activity. A classroom of two hundred students with theater-style seating presents what appear to be insuperable obstacles to small-group involvement, unless small groups move outside the classroom setting. In some courses, it might feel more natural to use groups—if the course plan has projects or presentations built into it, for example. But for all students, learning is enhanced when they feel directly a part of their learning. And groups encourage students to make themselves directly a part.

What Types of Group Projects Are Most Prone to Success?

Any activity can be successful in a small group, provided (see Maxim #4) that the activity is real. But some activities are more successful later in a term rather than earlier because students will be better able to collaborate when they have learned to know and trust their fellow members. Short, low-risk activities, especially creative ones, are good to begin with, and they develop a sense of communal spirit that can help when students engage in more difficult tasks such as making presentations or responding to drafts of papers. Projects that allow individual strengths to come to the surface—who's good at locating information on the Internet, who's good at coming up with an ending, who's good at creating an outline—help groups succeed in their work. Most of all, projects that engage students' interest will have a better chance of being successful than others will.

Students will sometimes need to meet outside class time to complete projects or plans for presentations, and these out-of-class meetings often present a problem. Students' schedules, like everybody else's, are tight. High school students have little out-of-class time during their school day and often have a host of activities and responsibilities outside class. College students have similar problems, often combining work schedules with class time, and increasingly, family responsibilities that make their on-campus time constrained. Students can be encouraged to meet right before class begins or before the school day to plan. And, with the growing use of email, students in a group can create their own list to conduct their discussions electronically. If groups are having trouble with time constraints, they need to be encouraged to talk with their teacher to help them find solutions. But teachers can design group projects so that most of the work can be accomplished in the classroom. Setting aside time in class for groups to work on projects is one important part of the course plan teachers design.

*   *   *

There are, no doubt, questions that I haven't answered, questions that grow out of your unique classroom context. I hope these questions and responses give you some help in puzzling out the others you might have as you engage in the process of putting groups to work.

Conclusion

All Right Everybody; Break into Your Groups

The word *break* carries a lot of connotations. A break is a relief. It's also something that causes a rift. The break makes a crack, a space. The classroom can be seen as a kind of circle, a circumscribed, finite line, that's meant to encompass everybody who's on the roll. Its boundaries seem clear to students. The teacher talks, the students listen. The teacher questions, a student answers. The small group literally breaks this big classroom circle, and when it re-forms, at the end of the small group's work or at the end of the class, the classroom is no longer the same. The big classroom circle has altered its lines. The teacher talks, asks questions, to find out what the small-group circles have discovered. The teacher wants to know what they know. The chance for real talk, real interaction, in the large classroom group improves, often dramatically, because suddenly students are the individuals who know. Over and over again in my classes, I've seen the difference that small groups make to the action of the class at large. Students talk, they laugh, they ask each other instead of me. They've broken the circle and re-formed it as they broke into their own circles and used these circles to re-form the larger ones when they come back to the classroom group.

"Man is not whole as long as he is single; he is essentially a possible member of society," C. S. Peirce said. "It is not 'my' experience but 'our' experience that has to be thought of, and this 'us' has indefinite possiblities" (Weiner, 1966, p. xx). Peirce, the philosopher and logician, was speaking of a method for making meaning and coming to understanding and knowledge. He understood clearly the power of the community, of the group, to test ideas and generate thought. Not the individual alone, but the "possible member of society," the one among others, can create the indefinite possibilities of knowing.

How do we as teachers nurture these possible members of society, the individuals who must make individual experience a part of the larger experience around them? James Baldwin (1998) seemed to speak directly to teachers as he talked about the communal process of coming to know:

None of us, black or white, knows how to walk when we get here. Not one of us knows how to open a window, unlock a door. Not one of us can master a staircase. We are absolutely ignorant of the almost certain results of falling out a five-story window. None of us arrives here knowing enough not to play with fire. Nor can one of us drive a tank, fly a jet, hurl a bomb or plant a tree. We must be taught all that. We have to learn all that. The irreducible price of learning is realizing that you do not know (p. 788).

As members of the teaching profession, we must come to know our power to nurture or blunt our students' hopes, the power we hold to teach planting trees or dropping bombs. As members of the human family, we are linked with our students, as we learn from others. The small circle of the group can help us, teachers and students alike, share with others what we know and, especially, what we don't. The power of the group can finally give us hope for the indefinite possibility of teaching and learning.

Works Cited

Alcott, Louisa May. 1994. *Little Women.* New York: Oxford University Press.

Alvine, Lynne, and Linda Cullum. 1999. *Breaking the Cycle: Gender, Literacy, and Learning.* Portsmouth, NH: Boynton/Cook.

American Association of University Women. 1994. "Higher Education: A Chilly Climate for Women." Report. Washington, DC.

Applebee, Arthur. 1996. *Curriculum as Conversation: Transforming Traditions of Teaching and Learning.* Chicago: University of Chicago Press.

Atwell, Nancie. 1998. *In the Middle: New Understandings About Writing, Reading, and Learning.* Portsmouth, NH: Boynton/Cook.

Baldwin, James. 1998. *Collected Essays.* New York: Library of America.

Barbieri, Maureen. 1995. *Sounds from the Heart: Learning to Listen to Girls.* Portsmouth, NH: Heinemann & Boynton/Cook.

Bartholomae, David, and Anthony Petrosky. 2000. *Ways of Reading.* Boston: Bedford/St. Martin's Books.

Berthoff, Ann E. 1981. *The Making of Meaning: Metaphors, Models and Maxims for Writing Teachers.* Montclair, NJ: Boynton/Cook.

Brooke, Robert, Ruth Mirtz, and Rick Evans. 1994. *Small Groups in Writing Workshops: Invitations to a Writer's Life.* Urbana, IL: National Council of Teachers of Education.

Bruffee, Kenneth. 1984. "Collaboration and the Conversation of Mankind." *College English* 46: 635–52.

Bruner, Jerome. 1986. *Actual Minds: Possible Worlds.* Cambridge, MA: Harvard University Press.

Cisneros, Sandra. 1991. *The House on Mango Street.* New York: Vintage.

Conrad, Joseph. 1993. *Heart of Darkness.* New York: Everyman's Library.

Cooper, Marilyn, and Michael Holzman. 1989. *Writing as Social Action.* Portsmouth, NH: Heinemann & Boynton/Cook.

Cushman, Ellen, Eugene Kintgen, Barry Kroll, and Mike Rose, eds. 2001. *Literacy: A Critical Sourcebook.* Boston: Bedford Books.

Dead Poets Society. 1988. Directed by Peter Weir. Hollywood: Warner Bros. 129 m.

Delpit, Lisa D. 1995. *Other People's Children: Cultural Conflict in the Classroom.* New York: W. W. Norton & Co.

Elbow, Peter. 1987. *Embracing Contraries*. New York: Oxford Press.

Elbow, Peter, and Pat Belanoff. 1995. *A Community of Writers: A Workshop Course in Writing*, 2d ed. New York: McGraw-Hill.

Emig, Janet. 1983. *The Web of Meaning: Essays on Writing, Teaching, Learning, And Thinking*. Edited by Dixie Goswami and Maureen Butler. Portsmouth, NH: Boynton/Cook.

Erickson, Bette La Sere, and Diane Weltner Strommer. 1991 *Teaching College Freshmen*. San Francisco: Jossey-Bass, Publishers.

Fetterley, Judith. 1978. *The Resisting Reader: A Feminist Approach to American Fiction*. Bloomington: Indiana University Press.

Fish, Stanley. 1980. *Is There a Text in this Class? The Authority of Interpretive Communities*. Cambridge, MA: Harvard University Press.

Flynn, Elizabeth, and Patrocino Schweikart, eds. 1986. *Gender and Reading: Essays on Readers, Texts and Contexts*. Baltimore: Johns Hopkins University Press.

Fox, Thomas. 1994. "Race and Gender in Collaborative Learning." In *Writing with: New Directions in Collaborative Teaching, Learning and Research*, edited by Sally Barr Reagan, Thomas Fox, and David Bleich, 111–22. Albany State University of New York Press.

Freire, Paulo. 1973. *Education for Critical Consciousness*. New York: Continuum Press.

———. 1984. *Literacy: Reading the World and the Word*. South Hadley, MA: Bergin Garvey Press.

———. 1985. *The Politics of Education*. South Hadley, MA: Bergin-Garvey Press.

———. 1994. *A Pedagogy of Hope*. New York: Continuum Press.

Gaines, Ernest. 1993. *A Lesson Before Dying*. New York: Alfred A. Knopf.

Gates, Henry Louis, Jr. 1988. *The Signifying Monkey*. New York: Oxford University Press.

Geertz, Clifford. 1983. "The Balinese Cock Fight." In *Local Knowledge: Further Essays in Interpretive Anthropology*. New York: Basic Books.

Gere, Anne Ruggles. 1987. *Writing Groups: History, Theory and Implications*. Carbondale: Southern Illinois University Press.

———. 1997. *Intimate Practices: Literacy and Cultural Work in U.S. Women's Clubs, 1880–1920*. Urbana: University of Illinois Press.

Gilbert, Sandra, and Susan Gubar. 1984. *The Madwoman in the Attic*. New Haven, CT: Yale University Press.

Golub, Jeffrey. 2000. *Making Learning Happen: Strategies for an Interactive Classroom*. Portsmouth, NH: Heinemann.

Griffin, Gail. 1995. *Season of the Witch: Border Lines, Marginal Notes*. Pasadena, CA: Trilogy Books.

Guterson, David. 1994. *Snow Falling on Cedars*. New York: Harcourt Brace & Co.

Heath, Shirley Brice. 1983. *Ways with Words: Language, Life and Work in Communities and Classrooms.* New York: Cambridge University Press.

———. 1998. "Ways with Words: Twenty-Five Years Later." Speech to the National Council of Teachers of English Spring Conference, April 10, 1998. Charlotte, NC.

Heilbrun, Carolyn. 1990. "The Politics of Mind: Women, Tradition and the University." In *Gender in the Classroom,* edited by Isaiah Smithson and Susan Gabriel, 28–40. Urbana: University of Illinois Press.

hooks, bell. 1994. *Teaching to Transgress: Education as the Practice of Freedom.* New York: Routledge.

———. 1999. *Remembered Rapture: The Writer at Work.* New York: Henry Holt & Co.

Hurston, Zora Neale. 1999. *Their Eyes Were Watching God.* New York: Perennial.

Kintgen, Eugene, Barry Kroll, and Mike Rose, eds. 1988. *Perspectives on Literacy.* Carbondale: Southern Illinois University Press.

Kozol, Jonathan. 1991. *Savage Inequalities: Children in America's Schools.* New York: Crown Publishers.

———. 1995. *Amazing Grace: The Lives of Children and the Conscience of a Nation.* New York: Crown Publishers.

Kramarae, Cheris, and Paula Treichler. 1990. "Power Relationships in the Classroom." In *Gender in the Classroom,* edited by Isaiah Smithson and Susan Gabriel, 41–59. Urbana: University of Illinois Press.

Kutz, Eleanor, and Hephzibah Roskelly. 1991. *An Unquiet Pedagogy: Transforming Practice in the English Classroom.* Portsmouth, NH: Heinemann & Boynton/Cook.

Labov, William. 1970. *The Study of Nonstandard English.* Champaign, Illinois National Council of Teachers of English, by special arrangement with the center for Applied Linguistics.

LeFevre, Karen Burke. 1987. *Invention as a Social Act.* Carbondale: Southern Illinois University Press.

Lunsford, Andrea. 1990. *Singular Texts/Plural Authors: Perspectives on Collaborative Writing.* Carbondale: Southern Illinois University Press.

———. 1991. "Collaboration, Control and the Idea of a Writing Center." *The Writing Center Journal* 12, no. 1: 3–10.

Maher, Frances. 1985. "Classroom Pedagogy and the New Scholarship on Women," *Gendered Subjects: The Dynamics of Feminist Teaching.* Edited by Margo Culley and Catherine Portuges. Boston: Routledge.

Maher, Frances, and Mary Kay Thompson Tetreault. 1994. *The Feminist Classroom.* New York: Basic Books.

Morrison, Toni. 1988. *Beloved.* New York: Plume Books.

———. 1992. *Playing in the Dark: Whiteness and the Literary Imagination.* Cambridge, MA: Harvard University Press.

Noddings, Nel. 1992. *The Challenge to Care in Schools: An Alternative Approach to Education*. New York: Teachers College Press.

Ogbu, John. 1988. "Literacy and Schooling in Subordinate Cultures: The Case of Black Americans." In *Perspectives on Literacy,* edited by Eugene Kintgen, Barry Kroll, and Mike Rose, 227–42. Carbondale: Southern Illinois University Press.

O'Reilly, Mary Rose. 1993. *The Peaceable Classroom*. Portsmouth, NH: Boynton/Cook.

Peirce, Charles Sanders. 1931–58. *Collected Papers,* vol. 2, edited by Charles Hartshorne and Paul Weiss. Cambridge, MA: Harvard University Press.

Peirce, Charles Sanders. 1966. *Selected Writings*. Edited by Philip Wiener. New York: Dover Publications.

Piaget, Jean. 1954. *The Construction of Reality in the Child*. Translated by Margaret Cook. New York: Basic Books.

Pipher, Mary Bray. 1994. *Reviving Ophelia: Saving the Selves of Adolescent Girls*. New York: G. P. Putnam's and Sons.

"Report Examines Minority Underachievement." 1999 (October 17). *Greensboro News and Record,* sec. A, p. 11.

Rorty, Richard. 1979. *Philosophy and the Mirror of Nature*. Princeton, NJ: Princeton University Press.

Rose, Mike. 1989. *Lives on the Boundary: The Struggles and Achievements of America's Underprepared*. New York: Free Press.

Rosenblatt, Louise. 1982. *The Reader The Text The Poem*. Carbondale: Southern Illinois University Press.

Sadker, David, and Myra Sadker. 1990. "Confronting Sexism in the College Classroom." In *Gender in the Classroom,* edited by Isaiah Smithson and Susan Gabriel, 176–187. Urbana: University of Illinois Press.

———. 1994. *Failing at Fairness: How America's Schools Cheat Girls*. New York: Charles Scribners' Sons.

Shaughnessy, Mina. 1977. *Errors and Expectations. A Guide for the Teacher of Basic Writing*. New York: Oxford University Press.

Smitherman, Geneva. 1977. *Talkin' and Testifyin': The Language of Black America*. Boston: Houghton Mifflin.

Smithson, Isaiah. 1990. *Gender in the Classroom: Power and Pedagogy*. Urbana: University of Illinois Press.

Stagecoach. 1939. Directed by John Ford. Hollywood: United Artists. 99 m.

Stowe, Harriet Beecher. 1880. *Uncle Tom's Cabin*. Boston: Houghton, Mifflin.

Tannen, Deborah. 1990. *You Just Don't Understand: Women and Men in Conversation*. New York: William Morrow & Co.

———. 1994. *Gender and Discourse*. New York: Oxford University Press.

Taylor, Jill McLean, Carol Gilligan, and Amy M. Sullivan. 1995. *Between Voice and Silence: Women and Girls, Race and Relationship*. Cambridge, MA: Harvard University Press.

Trimbur, John. 1989. "Consensus and Difference in Collaborative Learning." *College English* 51: 602–16.

Vygotsky, Lev S. 1978. *Mind in Society: The Development of Higher Psychological Processes.* Cambridge, MA: Harvard University Press.

———. 1991. *Thought and Language.* Cambridge: Massachusetts Institute of Technology Press.

Williams, Patricia. 1991. *The Alchemy of Race and Rights.* Cambridge, MA: Harvard University Press.

Wilson, Harriet. 1983. *Our Nig.* New York: Vintage Books.

Woolf, Virginia. 1953. *Mrs. Dalloway.* New York: Harcourt, Brace.

Index